HISTORIC.

ARLINGTON NATIONAL CEMETERY

Trace the Path of America's Heritage

CYNTHIA PARZYCH

With an introduction by James C. Bradford

gpp®

Guilford, Connecticut

An imprint of Rowman & Littlefield

Distributed by NATIONAL BOOK NETWORK

Copyright © 2015 by Rowman & Littlefield

Maps: Trailhead Graphics © Rowman & Littlefield
Historical map on p. 86 courtesy of the Library of Congress; interior map on p. 26 courtesy of the National Archives.

All photos courtesy of the Library of Congress, except for the following: Photos on pp. 13, 15, 23, 29, 35, 40, 84 (bottom right), and 85 (bottom) by C. Parzych; photo on p. iii from Shutterstock © Jason Gower; photo on p. 2 from Shutterstock © MISHELLA; photo on p. 9 from Shutterstock © A. McGuirk; photo on p. 12 from Shutterstock © David Kay; photo on p. 16 from Shutterstock © Jason Maehl; photos on pp. 69, 75, and 79 courtesy of Arlington National Cemetery; photo on p. 78 from Shutterstock © John Barry de Nicola; photo on p. 83 from Shutterstock © John Keith; photo on p. 84 (top left) from Shutterstock © Jeremy R. Smith, Sr.; photo on p. 87 (top) from Shutterstock © Stephen Finn; photo on p. 87 (middle) from Shutterstock © Zack Frank; photo on p. 87 (bottom) from Shutterstock © Frontpage; photo on p. 88 (bottom) from Shutterstock © Donald R. Swartz.

British Library Cataloguing in Publication Information Available

Library of Congress Cataloging-in-Publication Data Available

ISBN 978-1-4930-1300-5 (pbk.)
ISBN 978-1-4930-1750-8 (e-book)

∞™ The paper used in this publication meets the minimum requirements of American National Standard for Information Sciences—Permanence of Paper for Printed Library Materials, ANSI/NISO Z39.48-1992.

All the information in this guidebook is subject to change. We recommend that you call ahead to obtain current information before traveling. All restaurants are open daily for breakfast, lunch, and dinner, unless otherwise noted.

Contents

Graves at Arlington decorated for Christmas.

Introduction
by JAMES C. BRADFORD

The history of the estate upon which Arlington National Cemetery now rests is entwined with that of Virginia's early settlement and several of the first families of Virginia, to whom legions of genealogists seek to link their ancestors and those of their clients. Among the most prominent of these are the Custis, Lee, and Washington families, each of which traces the entrance of their progenitors into Virginia to the mid-seventeenth century.

The first members of the Custis Family to settle in Virginia established themselves on the colony's eastern shore circa 1650. Anne Custis married Argoll Yardley, son of Sir George Yardley, a former royal governor of Virginia, in 1649 and her brother, Dutch-born John Custis, accompanied the couple when they moved to America shortly after their marriage. Once in Virginia, John Custis established a plantation, which he named "Arlington," near the Yardley's home in Accomack, the first English settlement on the eastern shore of Chesapeake Bay.

A decade later, during the 1670s, John Custis replaced the dwelling house on his Northampton County plantation with a more substantial one that he called Arlington House. Constructed of brick, it was reputed to be the finest home in the Chesapeake Region. During Bacon's Rebellion (1676–77), a protest against Royal Governor William Berkeley's policies relating to land grants, the licensing of Indian traders, and protecting settlers from Indian raids in Virginia, Custis supported Berkeley, as did Colonel John Washington, the ancestor of George Washington. When Berkeley fled from Jamestown to the Eastern Shore he took refuge with John Custis at Arlington.

Daniel Parke Custis, John Custis's great-grandson, married Martha Dandridge in 1749; George Washington became her second husband in 1759. Dandridge's first husband was the father of John Parke Custis, who purchased 1,100 acres on the Potomac River in 1778 that he named "Arlington" after his ancestral home on the Eastern Shore.

When John Parke Curtis died in 1781, ownership of all the Custis family properties, including those on the Potomac River, passed to his infant son,

Arlington graves.

Arlington House.

TIMELINE ARLINGTON NATIONAL CEMETERY

1669	1778	1802	1831	1857
Governor Berkeley of Virginia gives Robert Hewson a 6,000-acre land grant that includes the Arlington property.	Arlington estate is purchased by Martha Washington's son, John Parke Custis, from Gerald Alexander.	John Park Custis's son, George Washington Parke Custis, begins the construction of Arlington House.	George Washington Parke Custis's only surviving child, Mary, weds Robert E. Lee at Arlington House, which becomes their home.	When her father dies, Mary Custis Lee takes control of the Arlington property.

George Washington Parke Custis, who, with his sister, Eleanor Parke Custis, went to live with Martha and George Washington at Mount Vernon and in New York and Philadelphia, while Washington served as president. In 1802, Custis reached age twenty-one and took possession of large estates,

George Washington at Mount Vernon.

including plantations in New Kent County and King William County in Virginia, and the Arlington property across the Potomac with its views of the White House and Capitol in the distance. Almost immediately upon inheriting the land, Custis made plans to build a large home on Arlington Plantation. In addition to serving as his residence, Custis intended that the house both provide display space for his collection of George Washington memorabilia and that it stand as a monument to his stepfather.

Custis engaged the English architect-builder George Hadfield to design and oversee construction of the edifice. Hadfield, who had supervised construction of the U.S. Capitol building between 1795 and 1798, sketched plans for a sixty-foot-wide central block with a twenty-five-foot-deep portico supported by six front and two side columns with Doric capitals, flanked by

1861	1862	1864	1866	1868	1872	1873
Robert E. Lee leaves Arlington, never to live there again; Union troops occupy the estate.	A tax is levied on the Arlington estate, and when Mary Custis Lee cannot appear personally to pay it, the property is auctioned off by the U.S. government, which subsequently purchases it.	Arlington becomes a national cemetery and the first Civil War casualties are buried there.	2,111 unknown soldiers from Bull Run and other battlefields near Washington are buried in a crypt near Arlington House.	The first Decoration Day (renamed Memorial Day in 1888) is observed at Arlington.	Uniform headstones begin to be used to mark graves at Arlington.	Mary Custis Lee dies.

Custis-Lee Mansion, now Arlington House, about 1900.

forty-foot wings on each side. Construction began with the North Wing in 1802, followed by the South Wing in 1804, and then by the central block, which was completed in 1818. Loggias were added to the rear of the house between 1818 and 1820. The structure then stood much as it looks today, but Custis ordered a variety of modifications for a quarter of a century, including, for example, surfacing of the portico with octagonal brick tiles in 1851 and the removal of the parapets on each wing.

1882	1883	1889	1892	1897	1899
Mary Custis Lee's family takes legal action for the return of Arlington; the U.S. Supreme Court rules that the government is a trespasser and that the property should be restored to the condition it was in when it was confiscated.	Custis Lee, son of Mary and Robert E. Lee, officially sells the Arlington estate to the government.	When the Freed-man's Village is closed by the government, Arlington annexes 142 more acres.	Revolutionary War dead from the old Presbyterian Cemetery in Georgetown are reinterred at Arlington, the first to be buried there from this war.	Fifty-six more acres of land are added to Arlington.	Spanish-American War dead are buried at Arlington.

George Washington Custis Lee (right), Robert E. Lee's son.

Custis experimented with a variety of crops and bred livestock on the plantation. In 1804 he wed Mary Lee Fitzhugh. The couple had four children, but only one, Mary Anna Randolph Custis, born in 1808, survived to adulthood. In 1831 she married Robert E. Lee at Arlington House. The Lees traced their Virginia lineage to Colonel Richard Lee, who immigrated to Virginia in 1639. Lee's father was the Revolutionary War hero Henry "Light Horse Harry" Lee of Stratford Hall in Westmoreland County; his mother was the great-great-granddaughter of Robert "King" Carter, reputed to have been the richest man in America when he died in 1732. The Lees were regular visitors at Mount Vernon and it was Henry Lee who eulogized President Washington

1902	1905	1909	1915	1920	1921
Spanish-American War Memorial is dedicated.	Unknown soldiers from War of 1812 are buried at Arlington.	Pierre L'Enfant's body is reinterred in front of Arlington House, overlooking the city he helped to design.	Construction of the Memorial Amphitheater begins; cornerstone is laid by Woodrow Wilson.	Memorial Amphitheater is completed and dedicated.	Unknown soldier from World War I is buried on the Memorial Amphitheater plaza.

as being "first in war, first in peace, and first in the hearts of his countrymen."
Thirty years later his fifth son, Robert E. Lee, wed Mary Anna Randolph Custis. For the next quarter of a century the couple made Arlington House their permanent home, sharing it with Mary's parents. Six of the couple's seven children were born in Arlington House.

During the second quarter of the nineteenth century, Arlington House was a magnet for Washington and northern Virginia society and its master, "Wash Parke Custis," was the host of frequent entertainments. All the while, the city of Washington rose on the opposite shore of the Potomac River. When Custis died in 1857, he left the property to his daughter for her lifetime, after which it was to pass to the Lee's eldest son, George Washington Custis Lee. At that time the main house was in serious disrepair, leading Robert E. Lee to take a three-year leave of absence from the army during which time he, as executor of his father-in-law's estate, directed a virtual rebuilding of many structures on the plantation and the reorganization of its finances.

Robert E. Lee returned to the U.S. Army in 1860, but at the outbreak of the Civil War the following year, resigned his commission and joined the Army of the Confederate States of America. Soon thereafter the U.S. government confiscated the 200 acres of the Arlington Plantation. Officers directing the construction of fortifications to defend Washington from the south made the Custis-Lee Mansion, today called Arlington House, their headquarters. Some of the soldiers doing the work were billeted on the property.

The U.S. government first took formal responsibility for burial of the war dead in April 1861 when the War Department ordered army commanders to designate cemeteries near every battlefield and assigned responsibility for the care of these burial grounds to the Quartermaster Department. A year

Arlington National Cemetery

1925	1930	1932	1933	1937	1945
Arlington House becomes a memorial to General Robert E. Lee.	President William Howard Taft is buried at Arlington.	Tomb of the Unknown Soldier is completed; Memorial Bridge connecting Arlington and Washington is finished.	National Park Service takes over the care and running of Arlington House.	A twenty-four hour guard is put in place at the Tomb of the Unknown Soldier.	The first prisoner of war casualties of World War II are buried at Arlington.

Union Soldiers at Arlington House, 1862.

later, on July 17, 1862, President Lincoln signed legislation authorizing the purchase of land to be used as national cemeteries. Procedures were not formalized nor were provisions made for moving bodies to centralized cemeteries until after the war, at which time there were fourteen national cemeteries. When nearby military cemeteries were filled with the dead from the battles at Bull Run/Manassas, Ball's Bluff, and other nearby engagements, the federal government purchased the remainder of the Arlington estate for "use, for war, military, charitable and educational purposes," in January 1864. The following June a portion was set aside for a new cemetery and the first bodies

1948
Integration of U.S. armed forces is declared by President Harry S Truman, dictating that segregation of burials in national cemeteries is no longer permitted.

1958
Unknown soldiers from World War II and the Korean War are interred at Arlington.

1959
In April, the one hundred thousandth burial takes place at Arlington.

1963
President John F. Kennedy is buried at Arlington.

1968
Robert F. Kennedy is buried at Arlington.

1976
Headstones of Medal of Honor recipients are highlighted with gold lettering.

Confederate Memorial.

were interred that summer. In 1873 Congress enacted legislation allowing any honorably discharged veteran from the U.S. Army or Navy to be interred in the National Military Cemeteries.

After Robert E. Lee died in 1870, his eldest son, George Washington Custis Lee, filed a suit in a Virginia court seeking return of Arlington, asserting that it had been illegally confiscated. Over a decade passed while the lawsuit wound its way through state and federal courts. In December 1882 the U.S. Supreme Court found in Lee's favor and ordered the property returned to him. Three months later Congress purchased the property from him for $150,000. Custody of the Custis-Lee Mansion was transferred to the National Park Service,

1980	1981	1984	1986	1988	1994	1995
The Columbarium for cremated remains is opened at Arlington.	General of the Army Omar Bradley, the last surviving five-star general or admiral, is buried at Arlington.	Vietnam War unknown is buried in the Tomb of the Unknown Soldier at Arlington.	The two hundred thousandth burial takes place at Arlington and construction of a new visitor center begins.	The new visitor center is completed and opens.	Jacqueline Kennedy Onassis is buried at Arlington.	Construction of memorial to Women in Military Service for America begins with a groundbreaking ceremony.

Graves below Arlington House.

a branch of the Department of the Interior, in 1933, and subsequently renamed Arlington House, and developed into a memorial to Robert E. Lee. Arlington National Cemetery, including the Tomb of the Unknown Soldier and the John F. Kennedy Memorial, and the West Point Cemetery at the U.S. Military Academy, are the only two cemeteries still under the care of the army. All others have been administered by the Department of Veterans Affairs since 1973.

Together these monuments, Arlington House, the John F. Kennedy gravesite, the Tomb of the Unknown Soldier, and Arlington National Cemetery constitute some of the most hallowed sites of American history.

1998	1999	2001	2002	2009
The body of the Vietnam Unknown is identified as Air Force Captain Michael Blassie and removed for burial in his hometown.	Congress authorizes thirty-seven acres of land from the Navy Annex and eight acres from Fort Myer for use by Arlington.	The National Park Service gives twelve acres of land to Arlington, increasing its size to 624 acres.	The private monument sections of Arlington become closed to new burials.	In January, the first phase of the Millennium Project is completed on the western edge of the cemetery with the construction of new gravesites and columbarium courts; the Secretary of the Army approves a new policy stating that all soldiers killed in action by the enemy and to be interred, inurned, or memorialized at Arlington shall receive full military funeral honors, including a caisson, band, and a military escort.

Key Figures

George Washington Parke Custis
The step-grandson of President George Washington purchased the Arlington property from the Alexander family. He built Arlington House and devoted his life to making the property a beautiful spot.

Robert Hewson
He received a grant of 6,000 acres of land from Sir William Berkeley, Royal Governor of Virginia in 1669, of which the Arlington estate was a part.

Mary Custis Lee
The only child of George Washington Parke Custis, the Arlington estate came under her control after her father's death in 1857. She married Robert E. Lee in the house in 1831, and they lived there until 1861, when he joined the forces of the Confederacy in the Civil War. She visited the property one last time in 1873 after the government confiscated her home and turned it into a cemetery, but was too overcome by emotion to enter the house; she died a few months later.

General Robert E. Lee

From 1831 until 1861, Lee lived in Arlington House and was the overseer of his wife's family property. The couple was married in the house and he and his wife raised seven children there, six of whom were born in Arlington House. Because of his Southern loyalties during the Civil War, the house and the land were occupied by U.S. troops when he left Arlington in 1861 to lead Virginia's military forces. Lee never returned to Arlington.

Quartermaster General of the Army Montgomery C. Meigs

The administrator of federal cemeteries during the Civil War, he considered Robert E. Lee a traitor. Meigs asked Secretary of War Edwin Stanton for permission to bury the Civil War military dead on the 200 acres comprising the Arlington estate and to make it a national military cemetery. His intention was to bury soldiers near the house, so as to make the property uninhabitable. Meigs and members of his family are buried at Arlington National Cemetery.

Arlington National Cemetery: A Historical Tour

It's somehow fitting that this beautiful spot on the Virginia bank of the Potomac, across a bridge from the nation's capital, has throughout American history been a national symbol. Situated on the old Georgetown and Alexandria pike that was the connecting route between two important colonial towns, the Arlington property rises on a hill above the Potomac with spectacular views of Washington, DC. Originally named Mount Washington to honor President George Washington, it was renamed "Arlington" by George Washington Parke Custis—a relative of the president by marriage—for Custis ancestral properties on the Virginia coast, to avoid the confusion from too many places being named for the first president.

At the start of the Civil War, the Arlington estate became a symbol of the divided nation, as this property belonging to Confederate General Robert E. Lee and his wife, Mary Custis Lee, was confiscated and used by Union Army forces assigned to defend the capital from Southern attack. As a payback for General Lee's Southern loyalties during the war, the U.S. Army buried Union as well as

Arlington National Cemetery entryway.

Confederate casualties of the conflict in Mrs. Lee's garden and along the road that led to General Lee's former family home on the Arlington estate, the property which eventually was to become Arlington National Cemetery.

Today this parcel of land is considered one of the country's most hallowed places, which receives the bodies of those who served their country and lost their lives doing it. It is a place where the military dead can be honored by the nation, no longer divided as it was during the Civil War, and where the American people can have the single focus of remembering the sacrifice these men and women of all beliefs and colors made for the nation.

About 4 million people visit Arlington National Cemetery every year. While tourists are welcome to walk among the graves and monuments of America's military heroes, there is ever present the sounds and images of the funerals of soldiers and the families and friends who come to bury their dead and pay their respects. About one hundred funerals take place here every week, Monday through Friday. Visitors to Arlington are asked to show respect for these funeral services. It should always be remembered that Arlington National Cemetery's main purpose, under the auspices of the Department of the Army, is to function as a national cemetery and shrine to those serving in the armed forces.

In recognition of the fact that the nation's most important military cemetery is also one of the main tourist destinations for visitors who come to Washington, excellent visitor facilities have been put in place here by the government.

A reminder to visitors.

Historical Tours

Arlington National Cemetery is a sprawling place with acres of well-tended graves and memorials, so a little planning is recommended before your visit, whether you have just a few hours or a full day to spend. It will help you to get the most from your trip to the national cemetery.

Every trip to Arlington should begin at the visitor center located just through the main gate on Memorial Drive. Visitor parking can be found near this building; check the Web site for parking fees (www.arlingtoncemetery.org). There is also an Arlington National Cemetery Metro stop served by Washington's subway trains. Arlington Tours, Inc. offers an interpretive bus tour stopping near the Ord & Weitzel gate, President John F. Kennedy's grave, the U.S. Coast Guard Memorial, General John Pershing's grave, the Tomb of the Unknown Soldier, and Arlington House. Check the link for tours for more information: http://www.arlington cemetery.mil/Plan-Your-Visit/Tours-and-Groups.

Exhibitions are staged in the visitor center, and information services, including assistance to help find grave locations, is offered by staff members working there. Maps and guidebooks can be purchased in the visitor center bookshop. In the building are public restrooms. The cemetery is open every day from 8:00 a.m. to 5:00 p.m. from October 1 through March 31. From April 1 through September 30, the hours are extended to 8:00 a.m. to 7:00 p.m.

ARLINGTON HOUSE

The history of the cemetery begins at Arlington House, the next stop after the visitor center on any visit to Arlington National Cemetery. Its gorgeous position, on Arlington's highest hill with views of Washington, DC, is reason enough to go there.

The house, which is undergoing restoration, and its immediate grounds are a memorial to General Robert E. Lee and a museum focusing on the life

The view of Washington, DC, from Arlington House.

The estate is situated directly opposite Washington, on the Virginia bank of the Potomac, and the Lee mansion, surrounded by luxuriant groves, is on an elevation of two hundred feet, so that it can be plainly seen from many parts of the city. On a bright, clear day the huge portico of the mansion, with its eight classic columns, stands out very distinctly, and one would hardly think there was a mile of water between the mansion and the city. The estate comprises 1160 acres, mostly good arable land . . .
—Hutchins and Moore, *The National Capital, Past and Present*, 1885

Arlington House in the spring.

of his family. Lee's loyalty to the state of Virginia and its Southern stance during the Civil War is the reason his family home and estate became a national cemetery during the war. The National Park Service offers tours during the hours when the cemetery is open. Check the Web site at www. nps.gov/arho/ for information.

If you stand on the elegant front porch of Arlington House, a low whooshing of Washington, DC, traffic usually can be heard if the day is calm, but your attention to the mesmerizing panoramic view of Washington beyond Arlington will inevitably be broken by the sound of horses' hooves against pavement, marking the beginning or end of yet another burial procession and tribute to one of the nation's honored dead.

Early History

The documented history of the Arlington estate begins in 1669, during the reign of the English King Charles II, when William Berkeley, the royal governor of Virginia at the time, sold 6,000 acres of land to Robert Hewson, who in turn sold all that land for "six hogsheads of tobacco." The Arlington estate was part of the property purchased from Hewson by the Alexander family, for which Alexandria, Virginia, is named. John Parke Custis, son of Martha Washington from her first marriage, purchased 1,100 acres of land in 1778 from Gerald Alexander for £11,000 of Virginia state currency. When Custis died it was passed to his son, George Washington Parke Custis—step-grandson of President George Washington—who had lived at Mount Vernon with his illustrious grandparents for most of his life.

George Washington Parke Custis was but six months old when the death of his father left him to the care of General Washington. From that time to the death of Washington himself, his life was spent principally at the home of the great patriot . . . The boy had played games with Lafayette and the other heroes of the Revolution upon the lawns of Mount Vernon.
—**K. Decker and Angus McSween,** *Historic Arlington,***1892**

George Washington with his family.

Custis left Mount Vernon to live in Arlington at the death of his grandmother, Martha Washington, in 1802, bringing with him family heirlooms, particularly objects that belonged to his famous step-grandfather. He was twenty-one years old and a very wealthy man when he came to live on the estate, as he had inherited all the Custis estates in Virginia and Washington. The beauty of the position of the Arlington estate was the reason he chose to live there. He began to build Arlington House about a year after he left Mount Vernon. A classic-revival house made of stuccoed brick and modeled on the Temple of Theseus in Athens, Arlington House was designed by George Hadfield, the architect who helped construct the U.S. Capitol building.

At about the time the house was completed, Custis married Mary Lee Fitzhugh: he was twenty-three and she was sixteen. Custis and his wife lived on the Arlington estate, where he farmed the land, planting orchards and crops near the Potomac. Large grazing fields were set aside for the Merino sheep from Spain that Custis began to raise in 1803. That same year, he organized a meeting at Arlington House, inviting farmers who were interested in bringing about improvements in sheep rearing and woolen manufacturing in the United States. In addition, he sponsored an annual Arlington Sheep Shearing Festival on the estate. Every year farmers gathered to compete on this day in various sheep competitions. The end of the festivities was marked by a dinner "consisting mainly of fish caught in the Potomac," hosted by Custis beneath his famous step-grandfather's campaign tent.

Sadly, sheep farming on the Arlington estate, like most of the other things Custis attempted to pursue in his life, was not a great success: the flock was gradually killed off by poachers and dogs. And the sheep festival held there eventually died out with the sheep.

Despite a marked lack of ambition and the fact that none of the pursuits in his life resulted in a career, Custis became a man much respected because of his relationship to George Washington. He was often invited to speak about George Washington, including before both houses of Congress, and invitations to Arlington, where Custis tinkered throughout his life, were coveted. This portrait of the man by K. Decker and Angus McSween from *Historic Arlington,* 1892, describes Custis and his life on the Arlington estate:

The term dilettante *describes his character exactly. He had some knowledge of art, and at his home in Arlington painted a number of pictures, principally of battle scenes, with Washington as the central figure. He was a graceful and forcible writer, but his literary works consist only of an imperfect series of papers on Washington, some fragmentary poems, and a few poor dramas. He was an orator capable of rare eloquence, but he never used this ability save at a few funerals or on some occasion where the duty of welcoming a guest or of praising a friend devolved upon him. Even as a farmer he was a theorist and a dreamer . . . But with all this, his character stands out, in the early history of the century, with great prominence, as that of a genial and accomplished gentleman, simple and modest in demeanor, unswerving in his integrity and friendships, a lover of all that was best in his fellow-men and in the institutions of his country. He was such a man as historians ignore but mankind bestows its reverence and affection upon.*

The Lee Family

Robert E. Lee wrote to Agnes Lee, the third of his four daughters, from Fort Mason, Texas, January 29, 1861:
I do not favor the use of force to maintain national integrity. If the bond of the Union can only be maintained by the sword and bayonet instead of brotherly love and friendship, and if strife and civil war are to take the place of mutual aid and commerce, its existence loses all interest with me.

One of the happiest occasions celebrated at Arlington House was the marriage of Custis's only child, Mary, to Colonel Robert E. Lee on June 30, 1831. Mary Anna Randolph Custis was born in the house in 1808, was married in the drawing room, and, because the bride preferred to live there, she and her husband took up residence at Arlington House with her parents. Six of the Lees' seven children were born in Arlington House and family correspondence shows that the house was always filled with energy and happiness while the Lees were in residence.

When Mary's mother, Molly, died in May 1853, followed by her husband four years later on October 10, 1857, they were buried side by side in the family plot near the house. The year his father-in-law died, Lee took over the care of the estate, which he, too, had grown to love.

Four years later, however, when Virginia seceded from the union on April 17, 1861, the Lee family's idyllic life at Arlington came to an end. When General Winfield Scott offered Lee the command of the U.S. Army, Lee considered it, but on April 20, 1861, he sent Scott his letter of resignation, which he wrote at Arlington after a sleepless night, thus ending a thirty-two-year career serving this country. That day Lee, his wife, and children left Arlington for Richmond, leaving behind most of their possessions, and the house in the care of their loyal staff of slaves. A few days later, Lee became commander first of Virginia's forces and later of all the forces of the Confederate States of America. He never returned to Arlington.

Government Takes Over

On the night of May 23, 1861, 14,000 Union troops crossed the river to occupy Lee's home and property in Arlington on orders from General Winfield Scott to prevent Confederate gunners from occupying this high ground across from Washington, DC, a perfect spot from which artillery could bombard the capital. The commander, General Irvin McDowell, converted the manor house into comfortable quarters for the Union Army.

In 1862 the U.S. government levied a tax on the Arlington property, about which Mrs. Lee was informed in 1864. Confined to a wheelchair, she sent representatives with the payment of $92.07, but the tax commissioner refused to accept the payment, insisting the tax had to be paid in person by the owner. The property was soon seized, auctioned off, and purchased by the U.S. government

Officers and staff at Arlington House, 1861.

Fort Whipple, June 1865.

for $26,800; the estate had been assessed the year before the Civil War broke out at $34,100.

Soon after the Union army moved to the Arlington estate in 1861, construction began on two forts on the grounds—Forts Whipple and McPherson—as part of Washington's defensive system during the Civil War. When General George McClellan became commanding general of the Union army, he moved into the manor house after General McDowell's disastrous retreat from Manassas in July 1861. He planned the army's spring campaign of 1862 from Arlington House. The officers of Fort Whipple, and later those of Fort McPherson, the earthwork located just south of the mansion, became residents of the tent city that began to develop on the hill rising above the Potomac.

Some of the tents also housed hospital beds and patients, victims of the Civil War battles fought near the capital city. By 1864, with the war continuing, there were fifty-six hospitals in Washington, DC, set up in homes, churches, warehouses, and schools converted to care for mostly the Union wounded. But when casualties rose, Arlington received the overflow. Patients were taken to the tent city at Arlington, where the clean air and green surroundings were thought to benefit recovery. Military personnel who did not recover, however, were taken back to Washington for burial, until room for bodies in the city's cemeteries began to run out.

When the Soldiers' Home Cemetery, the only military cemetery in Washington, had filled up with over 8,000 dead from the war, a decision needed to be made about what was going to be done with the growing numbers of military dead. This task was left to Quartermaster General of the Army Montgomery C. Meigs, the administrator of federal cemeteries during the Civil War, an intense workaholic, who was operating under great pressure. His office had received complaints from the public that soldiers killed in the war had not been given proper burials, a topic that could easily contribute to a lack of support for the war in the North.

Military graves in one of Arlington's special sections.

Decker and McSween, in their early history of the Arlington property, describe how President Lincoln invited Meigs, burdened by the weight of where he was going to bury large numbers of military dead, to ride out in a carriage to Arlington with him at the end of their workday on May 13, 1864. Meigs, believing Robert E. Lee was a traitor, "was angered at the happiness Lee must have experienced amid the beautiful surroundings of Arlington, and in his mind a resolution [about where to bury so many casualties of the Civil War]

The first person ever buried on the land that is now Arlington cemetery was not a soldier, but Mary Randolph, a direct descendant of Pocahontas. She was the cousin of Thomas Jefferson and of Mary Lee Fitzhugh Custis, George Washington Parke Custis's wife.

at once took tangible form. 'Lee shall never return to Arlington,' he said abruptly, turning to the President. 'No matter what the issue of the war may be, the arch-rebel shall never again enjoy the possession of these estates.' On common canvas stretchers, borne by members of a detail squad, were the bodies of several unfortunates who had died in the hospital tents [on the Arlington grounds] . . . Gen. Meigs asked, 'How many men are there awaiting burial here?' 'With these, a dozen, sir,' answered the sergeant, 'no bodies have been taken away during the week.' 'Set down the stretcher,' commanded the Quartermaster-General . . . 'Captain, order out a burial squad and see that all the bodies at Arlington are buried on the place at once.' Then walking a few paces away he pointed out the slight terrace bordering the garden of the mansion, 'Bury them there,' he said." The first bodies were interred that day, and thus became the burial ground that would evolve into Arlington National Cemetery.

Meigs was clever in that he knew there would be a public outcry if the bodies buried near the Lee family home were disinterred after the war. And burying the dead near the house was a guarantee that no Lee family member would ever want to live in the house again.

Eventually, those first bodies were quietly dug up and moved to the lower cemetery and replaced by those of commissioned officers, who were buried all along the terraces near Arlington House, their graves indicated by wooden markers. In the months that followed, the unidentified bodies of more than 2,000 soldiers who died in the Battle of Bull Run and other battlefields near Washington were buried in Mary Lee's rose garden. By the end of the war

16,000 dead were buried around the house.

Some might say that for Meigs, burdened with the unpleasant task of finding a place to bury so many dead expiring in and near Washington, choosing Lee's property as burial ground for the military dead was an act of vindictiveness. Meigs had lost a son in the Civil War, despised the South even though he was born a Southerner, and considered Lee a traitor. In 1864 Arlington officially became a national military cemetery.

Mary Custis Lee went back to Arlington in 1873 to visit the people who served her family when she lived at Arlington, but she was so distressed when she arrived by the rows of thousands of graves on the property that she could not leave the carriage in which she was traveling. When she died a few months after her visit, her will made the provision that if the estate were returned or if there was a payment for it by the government, the payment should be divided between her son George Washington Custis Lee and her daughters. G. W. Custis Lee sued the government and the result was that he was paid $150,000 for the property in 1883 and the property officially became the government's.

I learn that my garden laid out with so much taste by my dear father's own hands has all been changed, the splendid forest leveled to the ground, the small enclosure allotted to his and my mother's remains surrounded closely by the graves of those who aided to bring all this ruin on the children and country. They are even planted up to the very door without any regard to common decency . . . Even savages would have spared that place . . . yet they have done everything to debase and desecrate it.
—**Mary Custis Lee, 1866**

FREEDMAN'S VILLAGE

Set up for fugitive or liberated slaves in 1863, the Freedman's Village, remains of which no longer exist, was located at the southern end of what is now Arlington Cemetery and set up as a model village. As soon as word spread about this village that offered good air and country-like conditions in Arlington, freed men and women flocked to Washington for shelter and work there. Some of the

Freedman's Village with a view of the Potomac in the distance.

Map of Freedman's Village.

former slaves of the Lee family, who had resided on the Arlington estate went to live in the village after they were freed on December 29, 1862, when General Lee executed a deed of manumission. The village had about 3,800 residents during and after the Civil War and when residents died, they were buried in Sections 23 and 27, traditionally called the "contraband section," because the justification for freeing slaves during the war was that they were the property of Rebels and therefore "contraband," subject to confiscation. This area became the resting place for more than 3,000 Freedman's

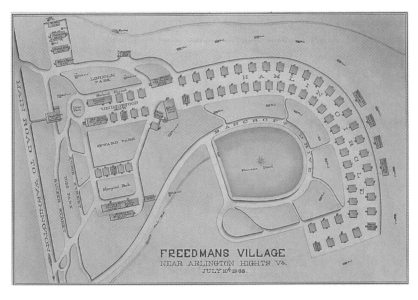

FREEDMANS VILLAGE
NEAR ARLINGTON HIGHTS Va.
JULY 10th 1865.

Village residents buried among the graves of African-American soldiers who served in the Civil War and subsequent wars. Their grave markers are simply labeled "Citizen" or "Civilian."

General O. O. Howard ran the village, set up on the Arlington estate in May 1863 and dedicated on December 4, 1863. More a camp than a village at first, it was intended to provide a temporary place for these people, but it sheltered freedmen for more than thirty years.

The exact location on the estate is not known, but it is believed to have stood near Sections 8, 47, and 25 along Eisenhower Drive. A series of tents initially, it provided housing (including facilities for the elderly and sick), schooling (there was a school-house, where students were taught to read), training in skills, religious services, medical care, and food. Abbott Hospital, started in 1866 in the village, had fifty beds and a staff of fourteen. Food consisted of army rations as well as wheat, corn, potatoes, and other vegetables that residents grew to feed them-selves and to sell for profit. Perhaps most impor-tant to the people living there was the protection from their former owners provided by U.S. Colored Troops, who guarded the village. In 1882, as sup-port for the former slaves began to fade, the U.S. Supreme Court closed the village and on December 7, 1887, the residents were given ninety days to leave to make room for more Arlington graves.

General O. O. Howard.

AFTER THE CIVIL WAR

When the Civil War veteran John Commerford became superintendent of the cemetery at Arling-ton in 1886, he was already faced at that early stage with the problem of space for additional burials. With about 19,000 bodies buried in the 200 acres of land the government purchased originally, and 300 burials annually, he was running out of space unless more land could be purchased.

Commerford requested permission from the Deputy Quartermaster of the Army in November 1887 to evict the African-Americans living on the property who were cutting down newly planted trees on the cemetery grounds for use as firewood. In response, the Freedman's Village that had been established on a portion of the Arlington plantation during the war was officially shut down and the cemetery expanded by 142 acres in 1889 and by another fifty-six acres in 1897, making Arlington the largest of the nation's national cemeteries.

Once the government officially took over the Arlington property, a sexton was appointed for Arlington National Cemetery and a substantial headboard was put in place to mark every grave from the early years. Between May 13 and June 30, 1864, 2,619 were buried in the cemetery, among them 231 "colored" soldiers. By June 30, 1865 (the war ended in April), 5,291 had been buried on the property. As time passed, everything possible was done to restore Arlington to its original natural beauty. The mansion became the superintendent's quarters. Drives were restored, lawns were cared for, and ornamental trees planted.

After the war, the important task of surveying all battlefields was begun on June 30, 1866, by Colonel M. G. Luddington and a team to identify bodies for reinterment and to try to identify all bodies in the battlefields of Maryland and Virginia within a radius of thirty-five miles from Washington. Members of the team walked the battlefields and when human remains were found they were placed in wooden cases. When their grim task was finished there were 2,111 wooden cases containing remains of unidentified soldiers. All were sent to Arlington for burial in a vault that was constructed on the site of Mary Lee's rose garden.

A granite sarcophagus was placed over the vault with the inscription:

> Beneath this stone repose the bones of 2,111 unknown soldiers, gathered after the war from the fields of Bull Run and the route to the Rappahannock. Their remains could not be identified, but their names and deaths are recorded in the archives of their country, and its grateful citizens honor them as of their noble army of martyrs. May they rest in peace.

By 1870, while work to improve Arlington continued, so did the burials. By the end of that year there were 15,932 graves on Arlington's grounds. Three entrance gates made of Seneca sandstone were constructed in 1871 and a grove of maples was planted in the southwest section, which eventually formed arched avenues. One of the gates

A more terrible spectacle can hardly be conceived than is to be seen within a dozen rods of the Arlington mansion. A circular pit, twenty feet deep and the same in diameter, has been sunk by the side of the flower garden, cemented and divided into compartments, and down into this gloomy receptacle are cast the bones of such soldiers as perished on the field and either were not buried at all or were so covered up as to have their bones mingle indiscriminately together. At the time we looked into this gloomy cavern, a literal Golgotha, there were piled together skulls in one division, legs in another, arms in another, and ribs in another, what were estimated as the bones of two thousand human beings. They were dropping fragmentary skeletons into this receptacle almost daily.

—The National Intelligencer

The granite sarcophogus that forms part of the memorial to the Civil War unknown soldiers.

was named for General Philip Sheridan, a second for General George McClellan, and the third for Generals Edward Ord and Godfrey Weitzel. The only gate that survives is the McClellan gate, made of red sandstone, which is not functioning, but has been saved for its historic significance. Ord and Sheridan are the only two generals in this group who are buried at Arlington.

The style of headstone now in use at Arlington was instituted in 1872: the original plain plank headboards were removed and replaced by slabs of granite. Between 1872 and 1892, a large section of the property west of Arlington House was designated for the burial of officers of the army and navy. A stone wall, required of all national cemeteries and put in place in the 1860s, was moved to encompass the old Fort McPherson earthworks, creating space of another one hundred acres for burials.

The Fort McPherson earthwork to the south of the cemetery was restored in 1892, the project of Superintendent Commerford; Arlington's landscape gardener; and fourteen laborers, all ex-Union soldiers, employed on the grounds. In addition, a single non-veteran, Wesley Norris, worked on the project. He was born on the Arlington estate and often accompanied George Washington Parke Custis on his hunting expeditions on the property. He was one of the family slaves who carried Custis's body to his grave at Arlington, west of the mansion.

Since 1864 more than 300,000 servicemen and many others who never served in the American military, have been buried on the cemetery's 624 acres. The passing of the World War II generation has recently created a great demand for burial

A caisson carrying a casket at Arlington.

space at Arlington—the greatest since the Civil War. It is estimated that burial space will run out in 2020. Today the rows of white headstones that seem endless are part of an emotional landscape that can be seen from Arlington House, where the history of this place began, set high on the hill that rises above the cemetery.

MEMORIAL AMPHITHEATER AND TOMB OF THE UNKNOWN SOLDIER

The Memorial Amphitheater was built as the setting for the services staged at the cemetery on Decoration Day, known today as Memorial Day,

Memorial Day 1929.

Laying the Memorial
Amphitheater cornerstone,
1915.

when members of the U.S. government, as well as the general public, pay tribute to the dead who served the nation. Many state funerals have also taken place here through the years. In 1868, General John Alexander Logan issued General

Order #11 that created Decoration Day, officially renamed Memorial Day by act of Congress in 1888, and declared a national holiday. The day was set aside so that the nation could honor veterans by decorating their graves, remembering those who served and died, and also the sacrifice of their widows and orphans.

These annual ceremonies attracted such large crowds to the cemetery that something needed to be done to accommodate them all. Congress appropriated money to build the Old Amphitheater that was finally completed in 1874 to accommodate 1,500 visitors. But the annual crowds continued to grow and by 1913 it was obvious that something had to be done, so Congress provided money that year to build the Memorial Amphitheater to accommodate 5,000 and ground-breaking ceremonies for its construction were staged in October of 1915, attended by President Woodrow Wilson, who laid the cornerstone. American participation in World War I delayed completion, but finally it was finished and dedication ceremonies were held on May 15, 1920, attended by veterans of the Civil War, Spanish-American War, and World War I.

Today the Amphitheater and the Tomb of the Unknowns on the plaza adjacent, which honors military personnel who have died in battle but whose identity is not known, have become the central focus of the cemetery for most visitors. A military guard or sentinel, each a member of the Third U.S. Infantry, familiarly known as "the Old Guard," stands watch over the tomb twenty-four hours a day, 365 days a year. He paces twenty-one steps; stops, faces the tomb for twenty-one

This is the *New York Times* account of the first Memorial Day at Arlington House on May 30, 1868, attended by General Ulysses S. Grant and General James Garfield:

The ceremonies consequent upon the decoration of the soldiers' graves at the Arlington National cemetery were most imposing and impressive. About 10:30 o'clock the Committee completed their labors, and four large army wagons were filled with evergreens of every description, and the Committee of Arrangements . . . proceeded to Arlington Heights . . . the flowers and evergreens were turned over to the Decoration Committee, who took charge of them until the time arrived for the decoration of the grounds. About the same hour throngs of people . . . started for the grounds. Some idea of the immense crowd may be formed from the fact that more than three hundred vehicles passed the Arlington toll gate en route to the cemetery, and it is estimated that at least five thousand pedestrians were present.

Historical Tours

Ceremonies for the burial of the Unknown Soldier of World War I, 1921.

seconds, and then turns sharply. After a click of his heels, he walks back and repeats this again and again, no matter the weather conditions or time of day.

Here Rests in Honored Glory an American Soldier Known But to God
—**Inscription on the Tomb of the Unknown Soldier**

In May 1984, the remains of an anonymous soldier from the Vietnam War were buried in the Tomb of the Unknowns. His remains lay in state in the Capitol building over Memorial Day weekend and 250,000 people came to pay their respects. Fourteen years later the Vietnam unknown was identified through DNA as Air Force Captain Michael Blassie, shot down May 11, 1972. His remains were removed by his family and taken to St. Louis for reburial.

A member of "the Old Guard" stands watch at the Tomb of the Unknown Soldier.

FINDING GRAVES AT ARLINGTON NATIONAL CEMETERY

We have compiled a selected list of graves of some of those buried at Arlington, listing them alphabetically with the section and grave number following their birthdates, and listing their names under the heading of the American war in which they either distinguished themselves or in which they are best known to have participated. The information desk at the Arlington Visitor Center can give you advice about locating precise graves using the grave numbers we have provided.

American Revolutionary War (1775–83) Graves

Most of the graves of American Revolutionary War military and government officials that you'll find in Arlington National Cemetery were originally located in the Old Presbyterian Cemetery in Georgetown. The bodies, and some of the original gravestones, were moved to Arlington in 1892 when the Presbyterian cemetery was demolished.

Lieutenant Hugh Auld (1745–1813) 2-4801

Auld served in the Revolutionary War in the Talbot County (Maryland) Militia, where he had the rank of First Lieutenant. Buried originally in his family's plot in Claybourne, Maryland, his body was reinterred at Arlington on April 11, 1935.

Lieutenant Colonel William Ward Burrows (1758–1805) 1-301-B

Born in Charleston, South Carolina, and appointed Major Commandant of the U.S. Marine Corps by President John Adams just after its formation in July 1798, Burrows fought in the American Revolutionary War with South Carolina troops. His service with the U.S. Marine Corps saw him serving first in Philadelphia and then moving to Washington, DC, to administrate the activities of that military branch and overseeing Marine missions during the Quasi War with France and the war with the Barbary States. Burrows left the military in March 1804. Many of the Marine traditions and its famous esprit de corps originated under Burrows' guidance. Originally buried in the Old Presbyterian cemetery in Georgetown, Burrows' remains were reburied at Arlington on May 12, 1892.

Joseph Carleton (1754–1812) 1-299

American Revolutionary War veteran Joseph Carleton served as Paymaster of the Army and Acting Secretary of War from 1783 to 1785. On November 13, 1907, his body was moved and reinterred at Arlington from Old Presbyterian Cemetery in Georgetown.

Lieutenant John Follin (1761–1841) 1-295

During the American Revolutionary War, Follin, serving in the Continental Navy, became a prisoner of war at age seventeen, when the ship on which he was serving—originating from the port of Bellhaven (today known as Alexandria, Virginia) was captured by a British man-of-war after a three-day chase. He was held in a prison for three years, first near Plymouth, England, then in Gibraltar, and for about a year more on board a British man-of-war near Gibraltar. Released through an exchange of prisoners when the war ended, he was transported to Philadelphia. From there, he walked all the way home to Virginia, surviving by begging for food. Follin, a religious man, spent the rest of his life farming. His body was reinterred, with those of his two wives, at Arlington on May 23, 1911.

Colonel John Green (1730–93) 1-503

Green served in the American Revolutionary War for more than eight years, commanding a company of Minutemen at the start of the war. Wounded at Mamaroneck, New York, in October 1776, he distinguished himself at the battles of Brandywine and Monmouth. General Robert E. Lee's father, Henry "Light Horse Harry" Lee, wrote about Green in his memoirs and described him as "one of the bravest of the brave." The Continental Congress presented Green with a sword for his "meritorious achievement." Originally buried at Liberty Hall, Culpepper, Virginia, his body was reinterred at Arlington, with the body of his wife Susannah, on April 23, 1931.

General James House (1761–1834) 1-297-A

All that is known of House is that he served in the American Revolutionary War. His body was reinterred at Arlington on May 12, 1892, from the Old Presbyterian Cemetery in Georgetown.

Major Pierre Charles L'Enfant
(1754–1825) 2-S-3

A French national who came to America in 1777, L'Enfant served as Captain of Engineers on the staff of George Washington during the American Revolutionary War. He was commissioned to design and plan the new American capital city of Washington, DC, in 1791. Difficult to work with, he was dropped from the project. His plans were modified and used, but he received only $2,394.00 for his contribution. He died a pauper in 1825 and was buried on the Digges Farm in Prince George's County, Maryland. On April 28, 1909, his body was moved to Arlington and buried with great ceremony in front of Arlington House, overlooking the spectacular view of the city he helped to

L'Enfant's tomb, left of the flagpole

plan. On the monument that marks his grave is a W. W. Bosworth engraving of one of L'Enfant's plans of the District of Columbia. "Few men can afford to wait a hundred years to be remembered," Secretary of State Elihu Root said in a tribute to L'Enfant. "It is not a change in L'Enfant that brings us here," he said. "It is we who have changed, who have become able to appreciate his work. And our tribute to him should be to continue his work."

L'Enfant's tomb.

After remaining unnoticed for nearly a century beneath the soil of an obscure Maryland farm, the body of Major Pierre Charles L'Enfant, the French engineer who remodeled the City Hall in New York City and designed the National Capitol, was today removed to the Arlington National Cemetery after an impressive ceremony at the Capitol. The body was taken under military escort to the Capitol, where it lay in State until the hour for the exercises. President Taft, accompanied by Mrs. Taft, was present. Vice President Sherman and Ambassador Jusserand of France paid tribute to the memory of Major L'Enfant and spoke of the work of the French officer, particularly as it affected the building of the City of Washington. Gathered about the bier were representatives of the Society of the Cincinnati, whose emblem was designed by L'Enfant.
—Evening Star, April 28, 1909

Brigadier General James McCubbin Lingan (1751–1812) 1-89-A

Born in Maryland, he was working in a Georgetown store when he received his commission in the army, nine days after the beginning of the Revolutionary War. He saw action at Long Island, York Island, and was wounded at Fort Washington. Taken prisoner by the British at Fort Washington, he was held on the HMS *Jersey* for three and a half years. After the war, he was appointed by George Washington to the position of collector of the Port of Georgetown and became a strong supporter of freedom of the press. He was killed by a crowd in Baltimore while defending a local newspaper, the *Baltimore Federal Republican,* which had taken an anti-war position at the start of the War of 1812. Among the thousands who attended his funeral was George Washington Parke Custis, who gave the eulogy. Originally buried at St. John's Church in Georgetown, his remains were reburied at Arlington on November 5, 1908.

Oh, Maryland! Would that the waters of the Chesapeake could wash this foul stain from thy character!
—Part of George Washington Parke Custis's eulogy to General Lingan

Brigadier General William Russell (1735–93) 1-314-A

An early settler in Virginia, Russell helped to draft the Declaration of Independence. He fought in Washington's army during the American Revolutionary War, commanding various Virginia regiments. When Charleston fell in 1780, he was captured by the British and held prisoner, but was exchanged, took part in the capture of Stony Point, and witnessed Cornwallis's surrender at Yorktown in 1781. After the war, he served in the Virginia House of Delegates. Russell County, Virginia, is named for him. He was reinterred at Arlington on July 7, 1943.

Caleb Swan by Charles Balthezar Julien Fevret de Saint-Memin.

Caleb Swan (?–1809) I-301-C

Born in Maine and a resident of Massachusetts, this American Revolutionary War veteran began his military career in 1779 as an ensign in the Fourth Massachusetts Continental Infantry. His remains were moved from the Old Presbyterian Cemetery in Georgetown and reinterred on May 12, 1892. He became paymaster of the U.S. Army on May 8, 1792, and held that position until June 1808.

Fourteen bodies of unknown soldiers and sailors from the War of 1812 were reinterred at Arlington in 1905 from the Washington Barracks when it was being renovated. It is speculated that these were people killed during the British attack on and burning of Washington, DC, during the war. The National Society of the United States Daughters of the War of 1812 funded a memorial stone that is located in Section 1-299, which was dedicated in April 1976.

Boy Scouts decorating the grave of the War of 1812 unknown soldiers on Memorial Day.

American Civil War
(1861–65) Graves

By the end of the Civil War in 1865, about 16,000 of that war's dead were buried at Arlington; 4,000 of these bodies were unknowns. Union soldiers were placed in sections in neat rows, with separate sections designated for African-American soldiers. The graves of African-American soldiers who served with the Union Army in the Civil War or other wars before the integration of the military are marked U.S.C.T., or United States Colored Troops. Three of these individuals received the Medal of Honor during the Civil War. Although Arlington Cemetery was planned to be a burial ground for Union soldiers, plenty of Confederate soldiers, many of whom died as prisoners of war in or near Washington, DC, are buried there as well.

In 1906 Congress authorized the construction of the Confederate Monument. Confederate soldiers were not offered the same memorial tributes

Confederate Civil War monument dedication, 1914.

and grave decorations as Union casualties of the Civil War, and this was thought to be a way of rectifying the situation and of honoring those who fought for the South. Made of granite and bronze, the handsome monument was dedicated in 1914.

Many of the 16,000 graves of Union dead are close to Arlington House and can be seen in the rows of white headstones called the "Field of the Dead," just down the hill from the house. A quick scan of the headstones reveals the massive toll the Civil War took on this country in lives sacrificed. There are 482 Confederate graves organized around the Confederate Monument, found in Section 16. The gray granite memorial in the garden of Arlington House contains the remains of 2,111 unknown soldiers from the Civil War.

Major General Frank D. Baldwin (1842–1923) 3-1894

A double Medal of Honor recipient, born in Michigan, Baldwin was awarded the first of these while serving in the Atlanta Campaign with the Nineteenth Michigan Infantry at Peachtree Creek, Georgia, on July 20, 1864, where he led his men under fire toward the enemy lines, then captured two officers and their standard. The second was given for distinguished gallantry in action in the American Indian Wars at McClellan's Creek, Texas, on November 8, 1874, where he helped to save two captives being held by Indian warriors. Baldwin is one of nineteen servicemen to receive this honor twice. He also served in the Philippines during the Spanish-American War.

Major General William W. Belknap (1829–90) 1-132

Born in Newburgh, New York, he graduated from Princeton and practiced law in Iowa, where he also served in the state legislature. At the beginning of the Civil War, he served with the Fifteenth Iowa Infantry, participating in the battles of Shiloh, Corinth, Vicksburg, Atlanta, and Sherman's March to the Sea. He became collector of Internal Revenue for the First District of Iowa after the war and in 1869 served as Grant's Secretary of War until 1876, when he resigned after corruption charges.

Major General William W. Belknap.

Belknap (center) and staff.

Private William B. Blatt (?–1864) 27-18

Serving with the Forty-ninth Pennsylvania Volunteer Infantry in the Civil War, Blatt was killed during the Spottsylvania Court House Campaign on May 13, 1864, and buried the next day at Arlington, making him the first battle casualty to be buried there.

Private William Christman (1843–64) 27-19

Serving with the Sixty-seventh Pennsylvania Infantry and only twenty-one years old, Christman had only been in the army for two months and had spent most of his time in the service in Lincoln Hospital in Washington; he died of peritonitis. He is buried in what was Mary Custis Lee's rose garden next to Arlington House, one of the first service-men to be buried at Arlington.

Major General John Lincoln Clem (1851–1937) 2-933

Major General John Lincoln Clem.

Born in Ohio, he signed up to fight in the Civil War at age ten, joining the Twenty-second Michigan Volunteer Infantry as their mascot. Officers chipped in to pay him $13 per month and he was allowed to formally enlist two years later. From the summer of 1862 he served as a drummer, showing great bravery at Shiloh, when a shell destroyed his drum. At Chickamauga he served as a marker and carried a musket into battle, which he used to kill a Confederate colonel who tried to take him prisoner during the fight, for which he was made a ser-geant. In 1903 he became Assistant Quartermaster General of the U.S. Army, but he is best known as the "Drummer Boy of Chickamauga."

Major General George Crook (1830–90) 2-974

Born in Dayton, Ohio, Crook attended West Point, graduating in 1852, and then served in the Civil War at Chickamauga, served with Sheridan in the Shenandoah Valley, and was captured in 1865, but exchanged a month later. He served in the Indian Wars in the battles of Powder River, Tongue River, and the Rosebud and is known best for his capture of Geronimo in Mexico in 1883. He was also known for his equitable treatment of the Indians in the West.

Captain Edward P. Doherty (1840–97) 1-680

A Canadian by birth, Doherty was one of three men from the Sixteenth New York Volunteer Cavalry who captured and killed John Wilkes Booth, President Lincoln's assassin, in 1865. He served with the Seventy-fifth New York Volunteers, when he enlisted in the Union Army, was captured at First Bull Run and held prisoner for two months. He distinguished himself as a cavalry officer later in the war.

Major General Abner
Doubleday and his wife.

Major General Abner Doubleday (1819–93) 1-61

Born in Ballston Spa, New York, Doubleday was a civil engineer for two years before he attended West Point, graduating in 1842. Serving in the Mexican-American and Seminole Wars, he was at Fort Sumter on the day that marked the beginning of the Civil War in April 1861, firing the first shot in response to the Confederate guns. He also served in the Shenandoah Valley, and at Second Bull Run, South Mountain, Antietam, Fredericksburg, and Chancellorsville. At Gettysburg, he took command of the I Corps when Major General John F. Reynolds was killed the first day of the battle. He is best known for being credited with inventing baseball, but evidence appears to show he never played the game and had no interest in it.

Major General Adolphus Greely (1844–1935) 1-129

Born in Newburyport, Massachusetts, he enlisted with the army and served with the Nineteenth Massachusetts Volunteer Infantry. In the Civil War, he saw action at Ball's Bluff, Antietam, and Fredericksburg. After the war he served in Wyoming, Utah, and Washington, DC, and volunteered for an Army scientific expedition to the Arctic in 1881, commanding a party of twenty-five men to set up a meteorological station at Ellesmere Island near the North Pole. This expedition, called the Lady Franklin Bay Expedition, established the Fort Conger base camp and weather station and discovered Lake Hazen and Greely Fjord. When supply ships failed to reach the group in 1882 and 1883, they broke camp and moved south, with no relief reaching them until June 1884, by which time Greely and six others were the only survivors. Greely continued his military career as Chief of the Signal Corps for about twenty years, overseeing the laying of telegraph lines and submarine cables in Puerto Rico, Cuba, the Philippines, Alaska, and other places, and also headed the U.S. Weather Service. Later in his career he oversaw relief operations after the 1906 San Francisco earthquake, retiring from the army in 1908. In retirement he took a trip around the world, helped found the National Geographic Society, and Washington, DC's first public library. In 1935 he was honored with the Medal of Honor on his ninety-first birthday for "his life of splendid service."

Major General Adolphus Greely.

Brigadier General William B. Hazen (1830–87) 1-15

Born in Vermont and raised in Ohio, Hazen attended West Point, graduating in 1855, served in the Pacific Northwest and Texas, and was severely wounded in 1859 in a skirmish with Comanche Indians, which put him on sick leave until 1861. He served in the Civil War as well, seeing action at Shiloh, Perrysville, Stone's River, Tullahoma, Chickamauga, Chattanooga, Knoxville, Atlanta, the March to the Sea, and in the Carolinas. After the war he served on the Western frontier, was sent to Europe to observe the German armies during the Franco-Prussian War, and was appointed chief signal officer by Rutherford B. Hayes in 1880.

Brigadier General William B. Hazen.

Oliver Wendell Holmes, Jr.

Brevet Colonel and Captain Oliver Wendell Holmes, Jr. (1841–1935) 5-7004

Born in Boston, Holmes served in the army during the Civil War with the 20th Massachusetts Volunteers and saw action at Ball's Bluff and Antietam; he was wounded three times in battle. After the war he taught law at Harvard, was a member of the Massachusetts Supreme Court for twenty years, and a justice of the United States Supreme Court for thirty years, where he became known as "The Great Dissenter."

Major General Philip Kearny.

Major General Philip Kearny (1814–62) Special Lot S-8

Born in New York City, Kearny graduated from Columbia University in 1833. When he inherited a million dollars from his grandfather in 1836, he immediately took up a military career, his dream since childhood. An accomplished horseman, he joined his uncle's regiment, the First U.S. Dragoons, in 1837, attended the training school for French cavalry at Saumur in 1839, saw action with the French in Algiers in 1840, and returned to the United States, serving as an aide to generals Alexander Macomb and Winfield Scott. He served in the Mexican-American War, where he lost an arm. He was killed after the second Manassas campaign near Chantilly, Virginia, when he rode into the Confederate lines. His body was taken to General A. P. Hill, who declared, "Poor Kearny, he deserved a better death than that." His grave is marked by one of only two equestrian statues at Arlington, a gift of the people of the state of New Jersey in 1914.

Major Jonathan Letterman (second from left).

Major Jonathan Letterman (1824–72)
3-1869

Born in Pennsylvania, where he was also educated, he was appointed assistant surgeon in the Army Medical Department in 1849, the year he graduated from medical school. He served in the Seminole Wars, at Fort Riley in Minnesota, and at Fort Defiance in the New Mexico Territory where he saw action against the Apaches. In 1859 he went to Fort Monroe, Virginia, and the following year saw action in the Ute Campaign in California. Assigned to the Army of the Potomac in 1861, he reorganized the army's medical service when he was appointed Medical Director of the Army of the Potomac in 1862. His new system of field medicine was put into action at the Battle of Fredericksburg in December 1862 and subsequently established officially by an Act of Congress in March 1864.

Letterman's headstone at Arlington reads:
Medical Director of the Army of the Potomac, June 23, 1862, to December 30, 1863, who brought order and efficiency into the Medical Service and who was the originator of modern methods of medical organization in armies.

Historical Tours

Lieutenant General Arthur MacArthur (1845–1912) 856-A

The father of General Douglas MacArthur was born in Massachusetts and served with the Twenty-fourth Wisconsin in the Civil War, fighting at Chickamauga, Stones River, Chattanooga, in the Atlanta Campaign, and Franklin, Tennessee, among other engagements. For the charge he led at the Battle of Missionary Ridge in 1863, he received the Congressional Medal of Honor. During his military career he also took part in the campaign against Geronimo (1885), the capture of Manila during the Spanish-American War, observed the final stages of the Russo-Japanese War in Manchuria, and served as military attaché in Tokyo.

Brigadier General, Brevet Major General Montgomery C. Meigs (1816–92) 1-1

The grounds about the mansion are admirably adapted to such a use.
—From General Meigs's June 15, 1864, letter to Secretary of War Edwin Stanton recommending that the Arlington estate become a national cemetery

Quartermaster General of the Army throughout all of the Civil War, some said the war could not have been won without him and his professional decisions about supply and logistics. His hatred for the Confederacy influenced his decision to make General Robert E. Lee's estate in Arlington, Virginia, a national cemetery. Born in Augusta, Georgia, but raised in Philadelphia, he attended the University of Pennsylvania and later West Point, graduating from the latter in 1836. Beginning his military career with the artillery, he was transferred to the engineer corps of the Army, where he worked for twenty-five years on projects including the Washington Aqueduct and the building of the wings and dome of the Capitol building. With Colonel E. D. Keyes he was secretly charged by

President Lincoln to relieve Fort Pickens, Florida,
which was achieved successfully in April 1861.
He is buried with his wife Louisa Rodgers Meigs
and other members of the Meigs family at Arlington. The grave of his oldest son, Lieutenant John
Rodgers Meigs, Chief of Engineers in the Army of
the Shenandoah, killed in battle in the Shenandoah
Valley in 1864, is located nearby with its distinc-
tive memorial sculpture consisting of a rectangular
block of black marble on which lies a bronze figure
of a soldier in full uniform with his revolver at his
side and impressions of horses' hooves around the
body, just as John Meigs's body was found.

Lieutenant General Nelson A. Miles (1839–1925) 3-1873

Born in Massachusetts, he attended night school
in Boston and educated himself in military history,
principles, and techniques. Serving in the Civil War
with the Twenty-second Massachusetts Volunteer
Infantry, he was a veteran of every major battle
fought by the Army of the Potomac except Gettysburg, including Fair Oaks (Seven Pines), Antietam,
Fredricksburg, and Chancellorsville, where his
actions led to his receiving the Medal of Honor.
The citation reads: "Distinguished gallantry while
holding with his command an advanced position
against repeated assaults by a strong force of the
enemy; was severely wounded." In fact, he was
wounded four times in the war. After the Civil War
he became a career soldier, serving in the Indian
Wars and the Spanish-American War, rising in
rank in 1895 to Commander of the Army. In 1903,
having reached the mandatory retirement age of

sixty-four, he received the distinction of being the last Commanding General in the history of the army. Tenacious in pursuing his beliefs, he aggravated many he served. Theodore Roosevelt called him "brave peacock."

Brigadier General Gabriel R. Paul (1813–86) 1-16

Born in St. Louis, Missouri, the grandson of one of Napoleon Bonaparte's officers, he attended West Point, graduating in 1834, and served in the Seminole and Mexican-American wars. In the Civil War he saw action at Chancellorsville and at Gettysburg. He was wounded at Oak Ridge when a rifle ball entered his right temple and exited his left eye, leaving him totally blind. He retired from the military in 1865.

Major General Wallace Fitz Randolph (1841–1910) 1-131-B-C

Born in Pennsylvania, he served in the Army artillery and became the head of it in 1901. There is a cannon mounted on his grave at Arlington, the only such grave marker in the cemetery. Shortly before his death he said that he had spent his entire life behind an artillery piece and wouldn't mind spending eternity under one.

Private Levi Reinhardt, who served with the Twenty-third North Carolina Regiment, was the first Confederate soldier to be buried at Arlington. Taken captive at Spotsylvania Court House, Virginia, on May 12, 1864, he was wounded in the leg, which was later amputated. He died from infection in Carver Hospital in Washington on May 30, 1864, at age thirty-nine. He was buried near the Confederate Memorial in Section 16.

Brigadier General Edmund Rice (1842–1906) 3-1875

Born in Cambridge, Massachusetts, after earning a degree from Norwich University in Vermont, he became an apprentice on the merchant clipper ship, *Snow Squall,* and headed to Shanghai in China. When he returned to New York in June 1859, he went to work as a surveyor for his father. He joined the Fourteenth Massachusetts Infantry in 1861 and saw action in many Civil War battles including Ball's Bluff, Yorktown, Fair Oaks, Savage Station, Glendale, Malvern Hill, Antietam, and Fredricksburg. For his actions at Gettysburg during Pickett's Charge he was given the Medal of Honor. He was present at the surrender at Appomattox Court House. He also fought in the American Indian Wars.

Major General James Brewerton Ricketts (1817–87) 1-17

Born in New York City, he went to West Point, graduating in 1839, and served on the Canadian border, in the Mexican-American War and in the

Major General James Ricketts (third from the left).

West. During the Civil War he saw action in twenty-seven battles. He was shot four times at the First Battle of Bull Run in July 1861, taken prisoner by the Confederates, and not released until January 1862. At Antietam, two horses were shot dead under him, the second injuring him when it fell on top of him. At Cedar Creek he took a bullet in his chest, disabling him for the rest of his life. His grave is marked by a granite stone on which is carved his military record.

Lieutenant General John Schofield (1831–1906) 2-1108

Born in New York and raised in Illinois, he went to West Point, graduating in 1853. He served in the Civil War, where he received a Medal of Honor for heroism. Superintendent of West Point (1876–81), he became Commander of the U.S. Army when General Philip H. Sheridan died in 1888. It was Schofield's suggestion to make Pearl Harbor in Hawaii a U.S. military base.

Lieutenant General John Schofield.

General Philip Henry Sheridan (1831–88) 2-S-1

Born in Albany, New York, and raised in Ohio, he attended West Point, graduating in 1853, and spent the early years of his military career on the western frontier. At the beginning of the Civil War, he served on the staff of General Halleck, Commanding General of the Army, taking part in the Corinth, Mississippi, campaign. After a defeat at Chickamauga, he led a victory at Missionary Ridge and was promoted to commander of the cavalry of the Army of the Potomac. He led the raid in 1864 in which Confederate General J. E. B. Stuart was

General Philip Sheridan.

killed at Richmond, Virginia. Sheridan was selected by Grant in the autumn of 1864 to lead a new military division into the Shenandoah Valley, where he defeated Jubal Early at Winchester Fisher's Hill, and Cedar Creek. He was present at the surrender at Appomattox Court House, Virginia. He took command of the U.S. Army in 1884 after the retirement of General William T. Sherman.

Corporal James Tanner (1844–1927) 2-877

Born in Richmondville, New York, he taught in local schools before the Civil War broke out. At the Second Battle of Manassas in 1862, he lost both legs, but he learned to walk again with two wooden prostheses. Desiring to continue to contribute to the war effort, he learned stenography and was employed by the Department of War. On the night of April 14 to 15, 1865, Tanner used his stenography skills to assist Secretary of War Stanton, working in the room adjacent to where President Lincoln lay dying in the Peterson House across from the Ford's Theater, in taking official statements from witnesses. These are the most accurate accounts of what happened immediately after the assassination.

Colonel John Wainwright (1839–1915) 2-1061

Born in Syracuse, New York, his family originally settled in Monmouth County, New Jersey, and had a long history of military service. He served with the Ninety-seventh Pennsylvania Volunteer Infantry during the Civil War, working his way from private to colonel in the same regiment in about four years after joining in 1861. He received the Medal of Honor "for gallant and meritorious services at the storming of Fort Fisher, North Carolina, January 15, 1865."

Lieutenant General Joseph Wheeler (1836–1906) 2-1089

Lieutenant General Joseph Wheeler.

Born near Augusta, Georgia, Wheeler graduated from West Point in 1859, saw service in the Indian Wars in the West, then resigned from the U.S. Army in April 1861 to join the Confederate Army, where he served with the artillery and later with the Nineteenth Alabama Infantry. From the Battle of Shiloh onward he served on the battlefield, was wounded three times, and had sixteen horses shot out from under him. He had a distinguished career fighting in many of the major campaigns of the war, but in 1865 he was captured near Atlanta. After the war he practiced law, grew cotton, and was elected to the U.S. Congress in 1884, where he served until 1900, rising to the position of Chairman of the Ways and Means Committee. At the outbreak of the Spanish-American War in 1898 he was appointed Major General of U.S. Volunteers by President William McKinley, and served in Cuba and the Philippines; the Rough Riders served under him in that war. He retired from the army in September 1900. He is one of only two Confederate generals buried in Arlington.

Brigadier General Marcus Joseph Wright (1831–1922) 16-0

Born in Tennessee, he practiced law and is best known as an author of histories and memoirs of the South, particularly the Confederate history of the Civil War. After the war he worked for thirty years collecting official Confederate military papers as an agent for the War Department. Appropriately, he is buried at the base of the Confederate Memorial, one of two Confederate generals buried at Arlington.

Spanish-American War (1898) and Boxer Rebellion (1900) Graves

The war declared by the United States against Spain on April 20, 1898, after the sinking of the battleship USS *Maine* in Havana Harbor in Cuba eight weeks earlier, brought more bodies of military for burial in Arlington. For the first time the bodies of soldiers and sailors who had fought on foreign soil were buried there. Just two years later, in May to August 1900, U.S. forces were sent to China to

Mast of the USS *Maine* in Havana Harbor.

The USS *Maine* Memorial commemorates the 260 men who lost their lives when the battleship exploded on February 15, 1898, in Havana Harbor, marking the beginning of the Spanish-American War. One of the masts from the ship was recovered, which serves as the main focus of the monument. Nearby are buried some of the men who died serving on the ship.

Burial of the dead from the sinking of the USS *Maine*.

relieve foreign legations from the threat posed by nationalist Chinese rebels in the Boxer Rebellion. Some of those who served in China are also buried in the cemetery.

Lieutenant General Adna R. Chaffee, Sr. (1842–1914) 3-1945

Lieutenant General Adna R. Chaffee, Sr.

Born in Ohio, he enlisted in the Sixth U.S. Regular Cavalry in 1861 and served in the military through-out the Civil War, seeing action in sixty battles including Antietam, Fredericksburg, Chancel-lorsville, and Gettysburg. After the war he served in the West and built a reputation as an Indian fighter, earning himself and the men who served with him in Texas the name of "Chaffee's Gueril-las." During the Spanish-American War in Cuba, he assisted in the capture of El Caney. After the war he returned to Cuba as chief of staff of the military government until 1900. Deployed to China with

2,500 men during the Boxer Rebellion, he led the troops that took the gates of Peking on August 14, 1900, thus calming the situation involving Chinese nationalist rebels in the city. In 1901 he became commander of the military district of the Philippines and received the rank of major general. In January 1904, he was named Chief of Staff of the entire U.S. Army. On March 4, 1905, he was grand marshal for President Theodore Roosevelt's inaugural parade. Retiring from the military in 1906, he moved to Los Angeles where he became chairman of the city's board of public works and president of the Southwest Museum.

Lieutenant Commander John McCloy (1876–1945) 8-5246

A double Medal of Honor winner and holder of the Navy Cross, McCloy was born in Brewster, New York, and joined the merchant marine at age fifteen. He received his first Medal of Honor while serving with the U.S. Navy in China during the Boxer Rebellion in June 1900, when "in the presence of the enemy, Coxswain McCloy distinguished himself by meritorious conduct." In 1945 as he was being honored in New York City for his service, he stated: "Every man [who served in the Boxer Rebellion] in the company deserved the Medal of Honor." A second Medal of Honor was awarded when he was serving in Mexico in April 1914 "for heroism in leading 3 picket launches along Vera Cruz sea front, drawing Mexican fire and enabling cruisers to save our men on shore . . . Though wounded, he gallantly remained at his post." In November 1920, while serving in World War I, McCloy was awarded the Navy Cross for distinguished service as Lieutenant Commander of the USS *Curlew,* a minesweeper operating in the North Sea.

Rear Admiral William T. Sampson (1840–1902) 21-S-9

Born in Palmyra, New York, he attended the U.S. Naval Academy, graduating first in his class in 1861, and later (1899) earning a degree from Harvard. He served on the ironclad USS *Patapsco* during the Civil War, which was blown up in Charleston harbor, the blast throwing Sampson into the water. He became superintendent of the Naval Academy in 1886 and held that position for four years. In 1898 he was president of the board of inquiry into the cause of the destruction of the USS *Maine* in Havana Harbor and, when war was declared with Spain, he commanded the 125 vessels that comprised the North Atlantic Squadron that finally defeated the Spanish fleet. After the war he commanded the Boston Navy Yard.

Rear Admiral William T. Sampson.

Major General Leonard Wood (1860–1927) 21-S-10

White House physician to President Grover Cleveland before the war, during the Spanish-American War Wood served as commander of the First Volunteer Cavalry, better known as the Rough Riders (future President Teddy Roosevelt was second in command). After the war he was military governor of Cuba until 1902. He also served in the military in the Philippines in 1904 and became Army Chief of Staff in 1905. In 1920 he was an unsuccessful candidate for the Republican presidential nomination. Then he served as Governor-General of the Philippines until his death.

Major General Leonard Wood.

World War I Graves (1917–18)

Over two million served with the American Expeditionary Force sent to Europe in World War I and 50,475 were killed during the war. The Argonne Cross, located on the southwestern side of the cemetery near a large section of World War I graves, is dedicated to the soldiers from the war that are buried in France.

Argonne Cross.

Rear Admiral Richard Byrd (1888–1957) 2-4969

Born in Virginia, Byrd graduated from the U.S. Naval Academy (1912) and learned to fly during World War I. He was involved in planning the flight path for the U.S. Navy's first successful transatlantic flight in a flying boat in 1919. He earned the Medal of Honor "for service on the occasion of the first flight of an aircraft over the North Pole," which took place on May 9, 1926. There has been considerable controversy ever since regarding whether he actually reached the North Pole. Byrd undertook five Antarctic expeditions between 1928 and 1956, and during World War II, he served as a consultant to the U.S. Navy.

Rear Admiral Richard Byrd.

Major General Adna R. Chaffee, Jr. (1884–1941) 3-1944

Born in Kansas and educated at West Point, graduating in 1906, he is considered the father of the armored branch of the military. A competent horseman, he first served with the Fifteenth Cavalry in the Army of Cuban Pacification, then went to Fort

Burial of the first World War I sailor at Arlington.

Riley, Kansas, to work with the Mounted Services School and commanded the mounted detachment of the Army War College. From 1914 to 1915 he served with the Seventh Cavalry in the Philippines and then returned to West Point as a cavalry instructor until 1917. During World War I, he served as an operations officer with U.S. forces at St. Mihiel and in the Meuse-Argonne Offensive and remained in Europe until 1919. He began the work for which he is best known when he served with the War Department's general staff (1927–1931) and began to develop a mechanized and armored force for the army. In 1931 he left that position to serve as the executive officer of the new First Cavalry (Mechanized) at Fort Knox. By June 1940, Chaffee was Commander of the Armored Force and worked to integrate all branches of the army into mechanized warfare. Sadly, he died in August 1941 before any of the major armored battles of World War II.

Major Louis Cukela (1888–1956)
1-427-A

Born and educated in Croatia, he came to the United States in 1913 and settled with his brother in Minneapolis. He enlisted in the U.S. Marine Corps in 1917, having previously served nineteen months in the U.S. Army. He served in France with the Fifth U.S. Marines and received from both the navy and army Medals of Honor for the same action on July 18, 1918. Advancing alone that day toward the German lines at Villers-Cotterets, he captured a gun by bayoneting its crew and then picked up their hand grenades and knocked out the remaining enemy. He took four prisoners and two machine guns. Upon retirement in June 1940, he was promoted to the rank of major, but he was recalled to active duty a month later, serving in domestic posts during World War II. He served nearly thirty-two years in the military, retiring finally in 1946.

Admiral William Leahy (1875–1959)
2-932

Born in Iowa, educated in Wisconsin, he attended the U.S. Naval Academy, graduating in 1897, and was assigned to the USS *Oregon* in the Pacific, participating in the Battle of Santiago during the Spanish-American War. He served in the Philippine Insurrection and the Boxer Rebellion in China, then, in 1902 in Panama during the early stages of construction of the Panama Canal. He served as an instructor at the Naval Academy (1907–09), served as navigator of the USS *California* in the Pacific Fleet, and was Chief of

Admiral William Leahy.

Staff to the commander of Naval Forces during the American occupation of Nicaragua in 1912. In World War I, he served on the USS *Princess Matoika,* which transported U.S. troops to France. Leahy became chief of naval operations in 1937, but retired two years later to become governor of Puerto Rico. President Franklin D. Roosevelt appointed him U.S. ambassador to France from January 1941 to May 1942. He was recalled to naval service in 1942 to serve as Chief of Staff to Presidents Roosevelt and Truman until 1949. He was made the first five-star admiral in 1944.

Lieutenant General John A. Lejeune (1867–1942) 6-5682

Lieutenant General John A. Lejeune.

Born in Louisiana, he received a bachelor's degree from Louisiana State University, Baton Rouge, and attended the U.S. Naval Academy, graduating in 1888. He entered the Marine Corps in 1890, and saw action in the Spanish-American War, Panama, the Philippines, and Cuba. During World War I he took command of the Marine barracks at Quantico, Virginia, and in 1918 was sent to Brest, France, to take command of the Second Division there until 1919, when he moved with his division into Germany. He returned to the United States in October 1919 as Commanding General of the Marine barracks at Quantico and was relieved as commandant in March 1929. He retired in 1930 to become superintendent of the Virginia Military Institute, a position he held until 1937. Serving with the U.S. Marines for more than forty years, he was known as "the greatest of all Leathernecks."

General of the Armies John J. "Black Jack" Pershing (1860–1948) 34-S-19

Born in Missouri, educated at West Point (graduating in 1886), Pershing was one of America's most famous and distinguished army officers from the period of World War I. He served in the Spanish-American War, the Philippines Insurrection, and the Mexican Expedition, where he led U.S. troops over the border to capture Pancho Villa. He was promoted to American Commander in Europe in World War I, in charge of the American Expeditionary Force (A.E.F.) that fought in France. The A.E.F. did not exist when Pershing received his assignment. He went to work at the difficult task of training a force of approximately two million soldiers in eighteen months to fight in France during World War I under the command of French General Ferdinand Foch. The prominent place that America holds in world affairs today is due in no small part to what Pershing achieved with those troops in helping to defeat the Germans during World War I. After the war he was appointed Army Chief of Staff. He retired from active duty in 1924. His state funeral service, attended by thousands of Americans, including members of the government and the military, was held at the Memorial Amphitheater at Arlington. He was buried in a simple grave near "his Doughboys" from World War I.

General John Pershing.

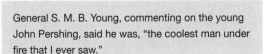

General S. M. B. Young, commenting on the young John Pershing, said he was, "the coolest man under fire that I ever saw."

Marine Corporal John Pruitt
(1896–1918) 18-2453

Born in Arkansas and raised in Arizona, while serving with the American Expeditionary Forces in France during World War I, Pruitt attacked two German machine gun positions with no support, killing two Germans and capturing German prisoners single-handedly. Later that day he was hit by mortar fire and died the next day. Posthumously decorated with two Medals of Honor, one each from the Navy and the Army, he was also awarded the Croix de Guerre by France and the Croce de Guerra by Italy, two Purple Hearts, and a long list of other honors. The navy named a destroyer, the USS *Pruitt,* after him.

General Charles P. Summerall
(1867–1955) 30-S-16

Born in Florida, he attended Porter Military Academy in South Carolina (1882–85), then West Point, graduating in 1892. He served in the Spanish-American War, in the Philippines, and then in China during the Boxer Rebellion. After six years as an instructor of artillery tactics at West Point, he served in France during World War I on the front line, eventually being promoted to Commander of the Fifth Corps. In 1926, he was appointed Chief of Staff of the U.S. Army, then was promoted to four-star general in 1929. He retired in 1930 after thirty-eight years of military service. In retirement he became the president of the Citadel, the military college of South Carolina, a position he held for twenty years.

World War II Graves

The greatest demand for space at Arlington for graves since the Civil War has been created by the generation of servicemen and women who fought in World War II.

General H. H. "Hap" Arnold (1886–1950) 34-44-A

General H. H. "Hap" Arnold's grave.

Born in Pennsylvania, he was assigned to the Philippines with the cartography division of the Army immediately after graduating from West Point in 1907. Taught to fly by the Wright brothers in 1911, he was one of the first military pilots in the world, despite a fear of flying, which he overcame. He oversaw the expansion of the military air services during World War I and commanded the Army Air Forces during World War II, overseeing its development and growth into the largest and most powerful in the world. President Roosevelt promoted him to the rank of Five-Star General of the Army in March 1946, and he was honored with the rank of General of the Air Force in 1949 in his retirement, making him the first and only person to receive five-star rank in two branches of the American military. He received a state funeral that included services held at the Memorial Amphitheater at Arlington.

Colonel Paul L. Bates (1908–95) 60-6101

Best known as the white colonel who refused to court-martial Jackie Robinson when the future Brooklyn Dodgers Hall of Famer refused to move to the back of a bus at Camp Hood, he commanded

Pappy Boyington's citation for his Medal of Honor reads:

. . . Consistently outnumbered throughout successive hazardous flights over heavily defended hostile territory, Maj. Boyington struck at the enemy with daring and courageous persistence, leading his squadron into combat with devastating results to Japanese shipping, shore installations, and aerial forces. Resolute in his efforts to inflict crippling damage on the enemy, Major Boyington led a formation of 24 fighters over Kahili on 17 October and, persistently circling the airdrome where 60 hostile aircraft were grounded, boldly challenged the Japanese to send up planes. Under his brilliant command, our fighters shot down 20 enemy craft in the ensuing action without the loss of a single ship. A superb airman and determined fighter against overwhelming odds, Major Boyington personally destroyed 26 of the many Japanese planes shot down by his squadron . . .

the first black tank battalion—the 761st—in World War II. Bates was born in Los Angeles, graduated from a Maryland college in 1931, where he was a member of the Reserve Officer Training Corps, and worked as a high school teacher and football coach before he entered the army in 1941. He took command of the 761st in January 1943, where all the enlisted men were black and separated off in segregated boot camps. When offered a promotion to colonel, which would mean he had to give up command of his battalion, Bates refused it. The battalion became part of General George Patton's Third Army that went into battle in Europe in November 1944, fighting without a break for 183 days. During that period it is estimated that this unit captured, destroyed, or liberated thirty major towns, thirty-four tanks, three ammunition supply dumps, four airfields, and a radio station; they also helped liberate Gunskirchen concentration camp. Bates retired from the army in 1963. He established a scholarship at his college in Maryland for descendants of members of the 761st Battalion.

Colonel Gregory H. "Pappy" Boyington (1912–88) 7-A

Born in Idaho, Boyington graduated from the University of Washington (1934) with an engineering degree, worked as a draftsman at Boeing, then joined the marines, where he was a flight instructor. He resigned to join Claire Chennault's Flying Tigers as a pilot in China. In 1942 he rejoined the Marine Corps, serving as commanding officer of Marine Fighting Squadron 214 in the Solomon Islands and in the Bougainville Campaign as a pilot. Shot down, rescued by a Japanese submarine, and imprisoned

by the Japanese in January 1944, the same day
he tied the Marine record of twenty-six air kills, he
remained a prisoner of war until he was liberated at
the war's end. He was awarded the Medal of Honor
when he returned to the United States. He retired
from the Marine Corps in 1947.

General Omar N. Bradley
(1893–1981) 30-428-1

Known as the "soldier's general" because of his
concern for the average soldier, he was born in a log
cabin in Missouri and graduated from West Point in
1915, in the same class as Dwight D. Eisenhower.
He served in World War II, first as a training officer,
and, then, in the European Theater under General
George S. Patton, Jr., before taking Command of
the Twelfth U.S. Army Group, the largest number
of American soldiers to ever serve under one field
commander. He commanded soldiers in North
Africa, Sicily, Normandy, and Germany. He headed
the Veterans Administration in 1945 and succeeded
General Eisenhower as Army Chief of Staff in 1948,
and became Chairman of the Joint Chiefs of Staff
in 1949. He was promoted to Five-Star General of
the Army in 1950. Leaving active service in August
1953, he pursued a career in industry, but maintained an active interest in the army.

General Omar N. Bradley.

Captain "Bobbie" Evan Brown, Jr.
(1907–71) 46-1021-17

Born in poverty in Georgia, Brown only completed the seventh grade and managed to enlist
in the army at age fifteen—he told the recruiter
he was eighteen—and remained with the army
for thirty years. In World War II he fought in North

Africa, then led a platoon onto Omaha Beach on D-Day. At Aachen, Germany, serving as captain in command of the Eighteenth Infantry Regiment's Charlie Company, he earned a Medal of Honor; the citation reads: "By his indomitable courage, fearless leadership, and outstanding skill as a soldier, Capt. Brown contributed in great measure to the taking of Crucifix Hill, a vital link in the American line encircling Aachen." The official army commendation states: "Although wounded by mortar fire he went forward and deliberately drew enemy fire in order to locate gun emplacements. He was wounded twice more but succeeded in securing information which led to the destruction of several enemy guns and enabled his company to throw back two powerful counterattacks with heavy losses to the enemy." Wounded thirteen times during the war, he also was awarded eight Purple Hearts. He left the army in 1952.

Lieutenant General Claire L. Chennault (1890–1958) 2-872

Suddenly. . . . we were being called the Flying Tigers. But the insignia we made famous was by no means original with us. Our pilots copied the sharktooth design on the P-40s from a colored illustration in the India Illustrated Weekly. *Even before that, the German Air Force painted it on some of its Messerschmitts. At any rate, we were somewhat surprised to find ourselves billed under that name.*

—General Claire Chennault

Famous as the leader of the all-volunteer Flying Tigers in China formed before World War II, he commanded the Allied Air Forces in the Far East. Born in Texas and raised in Louisiana, he went to college and became a teacher in a one-room schoolhouse in Louisiana, before he joined the military at the beginning of World War I. He learned to fly planes at Kelly Field in San Antonio, Texas, and was honorably discharged in 1920 after the war ended. But he joined the newly organized Air Service and was sent to Hawaii in 1923 as commanding officer of the Nineteenth Pursuit Squadron at Luke Field, Pearl Harbor. By 1936, he had become executive officer of another pursuit group at Barksdale Field in Shreveport, but retired because of disagreements with those in charge. In May 1937, now a civilian, he went to China as air adviser to the Chinese Air Force for the Nationalist Government leader General Chiang Kai-shek and his wife, Soong May-ling, during the Sino-Japanese War. When World War II began, he was recalled by the military and asked to continue the work he was doing in China, recruiting volunteers to fight the Japanese in China with his First American Volunteer Group, known as the Flying Tigers, beginning in 1941. The Flying Tigers became a part of the U.S. Army Air Forces in 1942. In 1945, Chennault once again retired from the military because of disagreements. He returned to China to start the Civil Air Transport to carry relief supplies into the isolated interior of China. In November 1958, just a few months after his death, Lake Charles Air Force Base in Louisiana, today known as Chennault International Airport, was renamed in his honor.

A Flying Tiger aircraft.

Field Marshall Sir John Dill (1881–1944) 32-S-29

Dill's role in World War II made him significant in developing "the special relationship" that formed between Britain and the United States during that period and which has since endured. Born in Ireland and educated at Sandhurst, he served with the British Army in the Second Boer War in South Africa, in France in World War I, commanded British Forces in Palestine (1936–37), was commander of the First Army Corps in France (1939–40) and then appointed British Chief of the Imperial General Staff in1940. Considering him too cautious in

His character and wisdom, his selfless devotion to the allied cause, made his contribution to the combined British-American war effort of outstanding importance. It is not too much to say that probably no other individual was more responsible for the achievement of complete cooperation in the work of the Combined Chiefs of Staff . . . We have looked to him with complete confidence as a leader in our combined deliberations. He has been a personal friend of all of us . . . We mourn with you the passing of a great and wise soldier, and a great gentleman. His task in this war has been well done.
—**The Joint Chiefs of Staff's message of condolence to the British military upon the death of Dill**

Historical Tours

74

that last position, Winston Churchill replaced him, making him the senior British representative on the combined Chiefs of Staff to Washington for the rest of the war. In that position, he proved to be a gifted diplomat. He died serving in that final position. His grave is marked with one of only two equestrian statues at Arlington.

Major General William J. "Wild Bill" Donovan (1883–1959) 2-4874

When President Eisenhower was told of General William Donovan's death on February 8, 1959, he remarked: "What a man! We have lost the last hero."

The only American to receive America's four highest military awards—Medal of Honor, Distinguished Service Cross, Distinguished Service Medal, and National Security Medal—he earned the nickname of "Wild Bill" in World War I. His Medal of Honor, earned in France, where he served with the 165th Infantry, Forty-second Division, was given, because "Lieutenant Colonel Donovan personally led the assaulting wave in an attack upon a very strongly organized position, and when our troops were suffering heavy casualties he encouraged all near him by his example, moving among his men in exposed positions, reorganizing decimated platoons, and accompanying them forward in attacks." When he was wounded in the leg by machine-gun bullets, he refused to be evacuated and continued with his unit until it withdrew to a less exposed position. Born in Buffalo, New York, during World War II he founded and then led the Office of Strategic Services (OSS), which led to the establishment of the Central Intelligence Agency. After World War II he served as an assistant to Robert Jackson, who was the Chief American Prosecutor at the Nuremburg War Crimes Trials, and he served as U.S. Ambassador to Thailand in 1953.

General James H. Doolittle
(1896–1993) 7A-111

Born in California, he was attending college there
when World War I began. He enlisted in the Army
Signal Corps as a flying cadet in 1917 and spent
the war as a flying instructor in the United States.
Completing his college education after the war, he
received both a masters and doctorate from MIT in
aeronautical engineering. When the war began he
saw service in the Pacific, leading the first carrier-
based bomber attack on the Japanese mainland
known as the Doolittle Raid, involving sixteen B-25
bombers taking off from the aircraft carrier *Hornet*
on April 18, 1942, for which he received the Medal
of Honor. His citation for the award reads: "With
the apparent certainty of being forced to land in
enemy territory or perish at sea, Colonel Doolittle personally led a squadron of Army bombers,
manned by volunteer crews, in a highly destructive
raid on the Japanese mainland." He continued
the war in North Africa, where he became Commanding General of the North African Strategic Air
Forces in March 1943, commanding the Fifteenth
Air Force in the Mediterranean theater in November 1943, and ending the war in command of the
Eighth Air Force in Europe and the Pacific from
January 1944 to September 1945. After the war
he returned to his job of vice president and later
director of Shell Oil. In March 1951, serving as a
civilian, he was appointed special assistant to the
Chief of Staff of the Air Force in March 1951, his
work there leading to the development of ballistic
missiles and the U.S. space program. He retired
from military duty in 1959, but continued to serve

James H. Doolittle's grave.

Historical Tours

the government as chairman of the board of Space Technology Laboratories. In 1947 he became the first president of the Air Force Association.

Corporal Rene A. Gagnon (1926–79) 51-543

Made famous as a participant in the Iwo Jima flag-raising, Gagnon was born in New Hampshire, completed two years of high school, and joined the Marine Corps in May 1943. He landed with his unit on Iwo Jima on February 19, 1945, and then returned to the United States to serve on a war bonds publicity tour. He served in China from November 1945 until the end of the war. He was discharged from the service in April 1946.

Fleet Admiral William F. "Bull" Halsey (1882–1959) 2-1184

Fleet Admiral William Halsey.

Born in New Jersey, he graduated from the U.S. Naval Academy (1904) and served on escort vessels during World War I and was awarded the Navy Cross for his actions while in command. During World War II he commanded the South Pacific Area in 1942 and led the first counter-strikes against the Japanese and helped launch the Doolittle Raid. Promoted to Commander in Chief of the Third Fleet in 1944, he provided support for General Douglas MacArthur during the invasion of the Philippines and won victories with his forces in the Solomon Islands, Okinawa, and other campaigns in the Pacific Islands. He earned his nickname from his favorite slogan, "Hit hard, hit fast, hit often." The Japanese surrender at the end of the war took place on the USS *Missouri*,

Halsey's flagship. He was the oldest person in U.S. Navy history, at age fifty-two, to earn his Naval Aviator's Wings in 1935 and one of only five men to have held the five-star fleet admiral rank. He retired from the military in 1947 and became president of International Telecommunications Labs, Inc.

Corporal Ira Hamilton Hayes (1923–55) 34-479A

A participant in the Iwo Jima flag-raising in World War II, Hayes was a Pima Indian, born in Arizona. After completing two years of high school, he worked with the Civilian Conservation Corps in 1942 and then enlisted in the Marine Corps Reserve. He was assigned to the Parachute Training School at Camp Gillespie in San Diego, and after he graduated, joined Company B, Third Parachute Battalion, Divisional Special Troops of the Third Marine Division, which sailed for New Caledonia in March 1943. He saw action with that unit on Vella Lavella, Bougainville, and Iwo Jima. Returning to Washington in May 1945, he was sent on a war bond selling tour, but received orders a few weeks later to return to the Twenty-eighth Marines to participate in the occupation of Japan. He was discharged from service in December 1945.

Major Audie L. Murphy (1924–71) 46-366-11

World War II's most-decorated combat soldier, Murphy was born in Texas and orphaned at age sixteen. With only five years of schooling, he enlisted in the army at age seventeen and was

Each grave at Arlington is decorated with a flag on Memorial Day.

assigned to the Fifteenth Infantry Regiment of the Third Infantry. He fought during World War II in North Africa, Sicily, Italy, France, and Germany. He earned thirty-three medals and awards during the war, the most prestigious being his Medal of Honor that he received for his actions near Holtzwihr, France, on January 26, 1945, when, according to a Pentagon record, "six Panzers and 250 infantry-men attacked Murphy's platoon . . . The lieutenant ordered his men to fall back to better defensive positions. He mounted an abandoned burning tank destroyer and sprayed the Germans with machine-gun fire . . . Though wounded in the leg, [he] remained at his position and killed 50 of the enemy single handedly. His actions delayed the German attack and enabled him to lead his men in a counterattack, which drove the enemy from the village." When he returned to the United States, he received a hero's welcome and his photo appeared on the cover of *Life* magazine. He spoke openly about his problems with post-traumatic stress disorder. He starred in an autobiographical film, *To Hell and Back,* as well as more than forty other films. He also wrote country and western songs. He died in an airplane crash in 1971.

Admiral Hyman G. Rickover (1900–86) 5-7000

Known as the "Father of the Nuclear Navy," Rickover was born in Makow, Russia (now a part of Poland) and came to the United States with his family in 1906. They lived in Manhattan and Chicago, and he attended the U.S. Naval Academy, graduating in 1922. He qualified for submarine duty and command and served on board two U.S. submarines between 1929 and 1933, and, then, on a minesweeper in 1937. He served as head of the Electrical Section in the Bureau of Ships during World War II. He was selected to head the development of America's nuclear submarine program. The result, under his direction, was the commissioning and launching of the world's first nuclear-powered submarine, USS *Nautilus* in 1954. Promoted to the rank of Vice Admiral in 1958, he was also awarded the first of two Congressional Gold Medals that same year for his work. Rickover was key in overseeing the American nuclear Navy for about the next twenty-four years. After serving with the U.S. Navy for more than sixty-three years and under thirteen U.S. presidents, Rickover was forced to retire in 1982. On July 21, 1984, the USS *Hyman G. Rickover,* a *Los Angeles*-class submarine, was launched in Rickover's honor.

Admiral Hyman G. Rickover's grave.

General David M. Shoup (1904–83) 7A-189

Born in Indiana, he graduated from DePauw University (1926), where he was a member of the Reserve Officers Training Corps. He served for a month with the Army Infantry Reserve and then was commissioned in the Marine Corps in 1926. In World War II, he served in Iceland; New Zealand, where he participated in training troops for the assault on Tarawa; and he was an observer on Guadalcanal. He earned the Medal of Honor "For conspicuous gallantry and intrepidity at the risk of his own life above and beyond the call of duty as commanding officer of all Marine Corps troops in

Although severely shocked by an exploding shell soon after landing at the pier, and suffering from a serious painful leg wound which had become infected, Colonel Shoup fearlessly exposed himself to the terrific relentless artillery, and rallying his hesitant troops by his own inspiring heroism, gallantly led them across the fringing reefs to charge the heavily fortified island and reinforced our hard-pressed, thinly-held lines. Upon arrival at the shore, he assumed command of all landed troops and, working without rest under constant withering enemy fire during the next two days, conducted smashing attacks against unbeliev-ably strong and fanati-cally defended Japanese positions despite innumer-able obstacles and heavy casualties.

—**From the Medal of Honor citation of David M. Shoup**

action against enemy Japanese forces on Betio Island, Tarawa Atoll, Gilbert Islands, from November 20 to 22, 1943." He served as twenty-second Commandant of the U.S. Marine Corps from January 1960 to December 1963, when he retired from the military.

Sergeant Michael Strank (1919–45) 12-7179

A participant in the Iwo Jima flag-raising, he was born in Czechoslovakia and raised in Pennsylvania, graduating from high school in 1937. He joined the Civilian Conservation Corps, where he worked for eighteen months, and then took a state job as a highway department laborer with the State of Pennsylvania. In 1939, he enlisted in the Marine Corps and participated in landing operations and in the occupation of Pavuvu Island in the Russell Islands, in the occupation of Bougainville, and then landed on Iwo Jima on February 19, 1945. He was fatally wounded while attacking Japanese positions in northern Iwo Jima. Originally buried on Iwo Jima, his remains were reinterred at Arlington in 1949.

General Nathan F. Twining (1897–1982) 30-434-2

Born in Wisconsin, he graduated from West Point in 1918, and served as Chief of Staff of the Army Air Forces in the South Pacific in 1942 to 1943. When the aircraft he was flying in was forced down in January 1943, he was left adrift at sea and rescued after six days. He commanded the Thirteenth Air Force in 1943 and later that year became commander of the air forces in the Southwest

General Nathan Twining (right) confers with General Patch (left) and General Harman after the Guadalcanal Campaign in 1943.

Pacific. He served as Commanding General of the Fifteenth Air Force in Italy and of the Allied Strategic Air Forces in the Mediterranean (1944–45). At the end of the war he became commander of the Twentieth Air Force, which dropped the first atomic bomb on Hiroshima. He served as Chief of Staff of the Air Force from 1953 to 1957 and then Chairman of the Joint Chiefs of Staff (1957–1960).

Lieutenant Colonel Matt Urban (1919–95) 7A-40

In addition to a Medal of Honor, Urban's heroism earned him seven Purple Hearts and many other decorations for his military service with the U.S. Army in World War II. Born in Buffalo, New York, he served with the Sixtieth Regiment of the Ninth Division in North Africa, Sicily, France, and Germany. According to the *1989 Guinness Book of World Records,* Urban earned twenty-nine medals during World War II, two more than Audie Murphy, who is generally thought to hold the record. The citation for his Medal of Honor, awarded in 1980, more than thirty years later because of lost paperwork, states that, while serving in France and Belgium, he " . . . distinguished himself by a series of bold, heroic actions, exemplified by singularly outstanding combat leadership, personal bravery, and tenacious devotion to duty, during the period 14 June to 3 September 1944 while assigned to the 2d Battalion, 60th Infantry Regiment, 9th Infantry Division."

General Jonathan M. Wainwright (1883–1953) 1-358-B

The son of an army officer and descendant of a line of distinguished naval officers, Wainwright was born in Fort Walla Walla, Washington. He graduated from West Point in 1906 and was commissioned into the cavalry, serving in Texas, the Philippines, and in the West. Promoted to captain after graduating from the Mounted Service School at Fort Riley, Kansas, in 1916, he was on the staff of the first officers' training camp in Plattsburgh, New York, in 1917. Serving in France during World War I, he was Assistant Chief of Staff of the Eighty-second Infantry Division and then went to Germany with the Third Army to assist in the occupation. During World War II he served in the Pacific and took command of the Philippine Division with responsibility for resisting the Japanese invasion that started in December 1941. Wainwright was promoted in March 1942 and took over the command of U.S. forces in the Philippines when Douglas MacArthur was ordered to leave Bataan. In April, the 70,000 defenders of Bataan surrendered and on May 5, the Japanese attacked Corregidor. The next day Wainwright surrendered

General Jonathan Wainwright in New York after the war, September 13, 1945.

to the Japanese to minimize casualties, and, by June 9, the Allied forces in the Philippines had all surrendered. Wainwright was held in prison camps for the rest of the war in northern Luzon, Formosa, and Manchuria, and was liberated by Russian troops in August 1945. He witnessed the Japanese surrender aboard the USS *Missouri* on September 2, 1945, and then returned to the Philippines to take the surrender of the Japanese commander. He received a Medal of Honor for his service in the Philippines. He was the highest-ranking prisoner of war in World War II and received a hero's welcome after the war. He retired from active duty in 1947.

Post–World War II Graves

Arlington National Cemetery is also the final resting place for military personnel who have served their country in all the modern conflicts, both large and small, since World War II including the Korean War, the Vietnam War, the Cold War, the Gulf War, Somalia, Afghanistan, Iraq, and others. Among those who served in the Korean War are the graves of Colonel William E. Barber, who commanded Fox Company from a stretcher during the Battle of Chosin Reservoir in 1950; General Creighton Abrams, Chief of Staff of the U.S. Army; General George S. Brown, Deputy Commander for Air Operations, U.S. Military Assistance

Color guard at Arlington.

Kennedy Family Graves

John F. Kennedy.

The eternal flame on the grave of President Kennedy, who served in the U.S. Navy in World War II and who was assassinated in November 22, 1963, was lit by his widow on the day of the president's funeral. Jacqueline Kennedy (later Jacqueline Kennedy Onassis), was buried next to him upon her death in 1994. Two of the couple's children are buried there as well. The idea of the eternal flame came from Mrs. Kennedy, who requested her husband's grave be marked with an eternal flame resembling the one on the tomb of the French Unknown Soldier in Paris. The president's brother Robert Kennedy, with Mrs. Kennedy's agreement, chose the slope below Arlington House as the burial spot, as it seemed ideal, being in a direct line as it was between the Lee family home above it and the Lincoln Memorial across the Potomac. President Kennedy had last visited Arlington House on March 3, 1963, and after the spot for the grave was chosen, a park employee pointed out that Kennedy had remarked on that last Arlington visit that he thought the house was so magnificent that he wished he could stay forever. The elliptical wall facing the grave is inscribed with quotations from Kennedy's 1961 inaugural address. Sixteen million people visited the grave in the first three years after his death.

Robert F. Kennedy, the brother of President Kennedy, is buried nearby, in a simple grave marked with a wooden cross, the only such grave marker in the cemetery.

The eternal flame at the grave of John F. Kennedy.

Robert F. Kennedy.

Robert F. Kennedy's simple grave at Arlington.

Command Vietnam, and later the Chief of Staff of the Air Force, and Chairman of the Joint Chiefs of Staff; General Daniel "Chappie" James, Jr., the first African-American four-star general to serve in the U.S. armed forces; General Roscoe Robinson, the first African-American Army four-star general; and General Earle G. Wheeler, Chairman of the Joint Chiefs of Staff, all served in the Vietnam War. Eighteen sailors who died in a fire on the USS *Forrestal* in 1967, those who died on the USS *Liberty* during the Six-Day War in 1967, and the marines who died in terrorist bombings in Lebanon in 1983 are buried at Arlington, as are the military dead from Operation "Just Cause" in Grenada (1983) and Panama (1989), the helicopter crewmen who died rescuing American hostages in Iran (1980), and sixty-four of the victims of the terrorist attack on the Pentagon on September 11, 2001.

Additionally, many non-military dead are buried at Arlington. Among these are President William H. Taft, nineteen astronauts, nine prominent explorers, sixty-three foreign nationals, four chief justices of the United States, and eight associate justices of the Supreme Court, all buried near Medal of Honor and Purple Heart winners, and those who gave their lives in conflicts serving the United States all over the world.

President William H. Taft.

Memorial to the crew of the U.S. space shuttle *Columbia*.

Arlington National Cemetery: A Tourist's Guide to Exploring, Staying, and Eating

PLACES TO VISIT NEARBY

Fort Hunt Park, located along the George Washington Memorial Parkway, six miles south of Old Town in Alexandria, Virginia, www.nps.gov/gwmp/fort-hunt.htm. Open sunrise until sunset, year-round.

Once part of George Washington's River Farm and the Mount Vernon estate, during the Spanish-American War the farm field became part of the area's coastal fortification system to protect Washington, DC, until the fort became obsolete in the 1920s. For a short time in the 1930s the fort's buildings were used as a hospital for war veterans, and from 1933 to 1938, the Civilian Conservation Corps worked there to transform the area into a recreation area. In World War II, it became a top-secret interrogation center for an estimated 3,400 German prisoners of war from 1942 to 1946. Today it's a popular place for picnics.

Map of Fort Marcy, 1871.

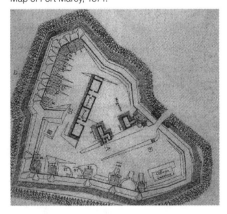

Fort Marcy, located along the George Washington Memorial Parkway, www.nps.gov/gwmp/fort-marcy.htm.

One of the five forts constructed during the Civil War to protect Washington, DC, what remains of the fort sits high above the Potomac and is now a public park through which visitors can wander.

National Air and Space Museum, Sixth Street and Independence Avenue, SW, (202) 633-1000, www.airandspace.si.edu. Open daily 10 a.m.–5:30 p.m. Free.

The most popular museum on the National Mall is packed with balloons, rockets, space ships, airplanes, and hundreds more artifacts dedicated to the history of aviation. The Wright Brothers' original Wright 1903 Flyer, the first successful plane ever built, is on display, along with Lindbergh's *Spirit of St. Louis* and the Apollo 11 command module that carried Buzz Aldrin and Neil Armstrong back to earth after the first lunar landing.

National Air and Space Museum.

National World War II Memorial, National Mall, Seventeenth Street between Constitution and Independence avenues, (202) 619-7222, (800) 639-4WW2, www.wwiimemorial.com. Open daily 10 a.m.–5:30 p.m. Free.

World War II Memorial fountain.

Fifty-six granite pillars are connected by a bronze, sculpted rope and symbolize the unity between nations during World War II. The Freedom Wall features 4,000 sculpted gold stars, which commemorate the more than 400,000 Americans who died fighting.

Netherlands Carillon, located on the northern end of Arlington National Cemetery, Arlington, (703) 289-2500, www.nps.gov/gwmp/historyculture/netherlandscarillon.htm.

A symbol of the friendship between the Dutch and Americans and a thank-you for the aid the United States offered the Netherlands during and after World War II, the fifty-bell carillon is adjacent to the U.S. Marine Corps Memorial. It was dedicated on May 5, 1960, the fifteenth anniversary of the liberation of the Netherlands from Nazi control. Check the schedule on the Web site for the times when you can hear the beautiful bells.

Netherlands Carillon.

Marine Corps War Memorial.

U.S. Marine Corps War Memorial, located on the northern end of Arlington National Cemetery, www .nps.gov/gwmp/historyculture/usmcwarmemorial .htm. Open 24 hours. Free.

Dedicated to all Marines who have served since the founding of that branch of military service in 1775, the memorial's statue depicts the famous flag-raising scene, captured by news photographer Joe Rosenthal on the Pacific island of Iwo Jima in February 1945, as Mount Suribachi was taken from the Japanese by U.S. troops. The memorial was begun and dedicated in 1954.

Vietnam Veterans Memorial, National Mall near Constitution and Twenty-first Street, (202) 426-6841, www.nps.gov/vive. Open 24 hours. Free.

More than 58,000 names of dead or missing servicemen and women are inscribed along "The Wall" or Vietnam Veterans Memorial, consisting of two large black granite slabs built into the landscape and rising toward each other. As a young student at Yale in 1980, Maya Ying Lin designed the monument and its surface to reflect the image of the viewer for a poignant reminder of the human sacrifice in Vietnam.

Vietnam Veterans Memorial.

HOTELS

You'll find many of the familiar hotel and motel chains represented on the Arlington side of the Potomac. One of these is a great choice for the night if you must limit your visit to Arlington National Cemetery or if you have time for only a short trip to the area. There are plenty of hotels of all types in Washington, DC, just a short journey by public transport or taxi from Arlington. The list below suggests a few which are comfortable or at a reasonable proximity from Arlington National Cemetery.

The Dupont Circle Hotel, 1500 New Hampshire Avenue NW, (202) 483-6000, www.doylecollection.com/hotels/the-dupont-circle-hotel.

Overlooking Dupont Circle, it's comfortable, modern, and located in a great neighborhood for strolling. Look out for its affordable package deals.

Henley Park Hotel, 926 Massachusetts Avenue NW, (800) 491-9657, www. henleypark.com.

There's nothing sterile about this aging charmer of a hotel, only a ten-minute walk from the White House. The rooms are well appointed and the staff is friendly and helpful. The English tea with scones and sandwiches is excellent. The bar and restaurant are warm, with a great deal of charm.

Hotel Rouge, 1315 Sixteenth Street NW, (202) 232-8000, www.rougehotel.com.

Although it looks a little drab on the outside, the rooms are spacious, comfortable, and stylish. The neighborhood is quiet with anything you might need just a short walk away. There's a wine reception for guests in the evening.

Hotel Washington, 515 Fifteenth Street NW, (202) 638-5900, www .hotelwashington.com.

There's a great view of the White House from its restaurant and bar on the roof. This is an older hotel—it's the oldest continuously operating hotel in the city—with rooms that are on the small side, but they are comfortable, warmly decorated, and quiet. Great place to stay for sightseeing with everything nearby.

RESTAURANTS

Central, 1001 Pennsylvania Avenue, NW, Washington, DC, (202) 626-0015, www.centralmichelrichard.com. No breakfast.

Dine on traditional American favorites with a touch of French perfection, such as the lobster burger, crispy fried chicken with mustard sauce, and fish and chips.

CityZen, 1330 Maryland Avenue, SW, Washington, DC, (202) 554-8588, www .mandarinoriental.com/washington. No breakfast or lunch, closed Sun–Mon.

In this restaurant within the Mandarin Oriental hotel, master chef Eric Ziebold has created one of DC's most memorable dining experiences.

Choose the six-course chef's tasting menu, which includes chilled Maine lobster consomme with Maryland crab cake, black bass, and pan roasted lamb.

Eamonn's Dublin Chipper, 728 King Street, Alexandria, (703) 299-8384, www.eamonnsdublinchipper.com. No breakfast.

Husband and wife team Cathal and Meshelle Armstrong have given new meaning to the saying "Thanks Be to Cod," with their traditional Irish chipper, featuring classic batter burgers (sans buns), cod, baked beans, and mushy peas.

The Liberty Tavern, 3195 Wilson Boulevard, Arlington, (703) 465-9360, www.thelibertytavern.com. No breakfast but brunch served on Saturday and Sunday.

A two-story neighborhood place, it serves excellent pizzas and other dishes cooked in its wood oven. The selection of beers and wines by the glass is terrific. The downstairs bar is noisy. It often caters receptions following memorials and burials at Arlington.

Tallula Restaurant, 2761 Washington Boulevard, Arlington, (703) 778-5051, www.tallularestaurant.com. No breakfast, no lunch, but brunch served on Sunday. Closed on Monday.

Seasonal ingredients, strong flavors, a fun wine list, and excellent selection of cheeses make Tallula a great place to seek out for a meal in Arlington.

Willow Restaurant, 4301 North Fairfax Drive, Arlington, (703) 465-8800, www.willowva.com. No breakfast; no lunch Saturday; closed Sunday.

The cooking is warm and welcoming, as is the beautiful interior of the restaurant. It's a great place to recharge after a full day at Arlington.

Glossary

artillery: Large-caliber guns; also the unit of the military that uses those guns.

columbarium: A building or room where funeral urns are stored.

Doughboy: A U.S. infantryman.

earthwork: A large, artificial bank of soil to be used as a defense.

eulogy: A speech or writing that praises someone who has died.

heirloom: An object that has belonged to a family for generations.

leatherneck: A U.S. marine.

man-of-war: An armed sailing ship.

manumission: The release of someone from slavery.

poacher: Someone who hunts or fishes illegally.

sarcophagus: A stone coffin.

Bibliography

Bigler, Philip. *In Honored Glory: Arlington National Cemetery, The Final Post.* 4th edition, St. Petersburg, Fla.: Vandamere Press, 2005.

Blair, William. *Cities of the Dead: Contesting the Memory of the Civil War in the South, 1865–1914.* Chapel Hill: University of North Carolina, 2003.

Decker, K. and Angus McSween. *Historic Arlington.* Washington, DC: The Decker and McSween Publishing Company, 1892.

Dodge, George and Kim B. *Arlington National Cemetery.* Dover, N.H.: Arcadia Publishing, 2006.

Gurney, Gene. *Arlington National Cemetery.* New York: Crown Publishers, Inc., 1965.

Hutchins, Stilson and Joseph West Moore. *The National Capital, Past and Present.* Washington, DC: The Post Publishing Company, 1885.

Peters, James Edward. *Arlington National Cemetery: Shrine to America's Heroes.* Arlington, Va.: Woodbine House, 2008.

Poole, Robert M. *On Hallowed Ground: The Story of Arlington National Cemetery.* New York: Walker & Company, 2010.

Poole, Robert M. *Section 60: Arlington National Cemetery: Where War Comes Home.* New York: Bloomsbury USA, 2014.

www.arlingtoncemetery.net

www.arlingtoncemetery.org

Index

Arlington National Cemetery